The Potato Cookbook

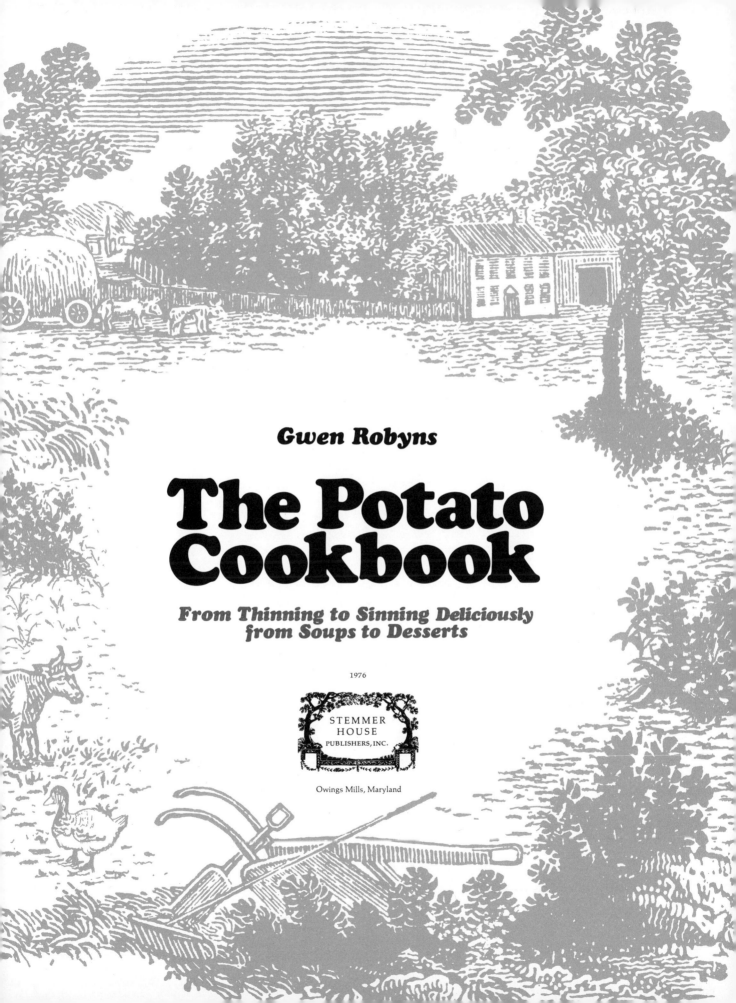

Gwen Robyns

The Potato Cookbook

*From Thinning to Sinning Deliciously
from Soups to Desserts*

1976

STEMMER
HOUSE
PUBLISHERS, INC.

Owings Mills, Maryland

An earlier, smaller edition appeared under the title *The Friendly Potato and a Cook Book,* © Gwen Robyns 1974, published in Great Britain by Keith Reid Ltd.

Illustration Credits:
The publisher wishes to thank the following sources for permission to use the illustrations herein: on page 107, the antique cut collection of The Artichoke Press, Bev and Stu Dobson, Proprietors, Irvington, N.Y.; 7, 42, The Bettmann Archive; 21, the Brighton Museum; 17, 18, The British Museum; frontispiece, 13 (*Parmentier showing his first crop of potatoes to Louis XVI*), 39 (*Woman preparing potatoes*), Culver Pictures; 97, 101, Grosvenor Arts Ltd.; 55, the Idaho Potato Commission; opp. 96, opp. 128, opp. 129, United Fresh Fruit and Vegetable Association; 19 (Van Gogh: *The Potato Eaters,* #30-820), owner, Kroeller Mueller Museum in Otterloo, Holland, photo credit, Peter Adelberg, New York, N.Y. 10023; cover, 25, 26, opp. 80, 81, 97, 112, 113, The Potato Board, U.S.A.; 10 (1633 edition of Gerrard's *Herball*), 15 (*Attack on a potato store,* Ireland 1842), 16 (A starving boy and girl, Ireland 1847), 22, 66, 128 (from Gerrard's *Herball*), The Potato Marketing Board, London; 28 (*Colorado Beetle costume,* 1877), 30, 93 (*Harrowing the potato crop, 1871*), 102 (*Searching for potatoes in a stubble field in Ireland*), Radio Times Hulton Picture Library; 117, Edward A. Tanner, A.R.P.S.; 23, 61 (*Harvesting potatoes in Aroostock, Maine, Sept. 1908*), 86, U.S. Department of Agriculture Photos; 20 (*silver potato ring*), Victoria and Albert Museum; 78, Hugh White Studios Ltd., photograph by John Challis.

Inquiries are to be directed to
STEMMER HOUSE PUBLISHERS, INC.
2627 Caves Road, Owings Mills,
Maryland 21117

A Barbara Holdridge Book
Printed and bound in the United States of America
First Edition

Library of Congress Cataloging in Publication Data
Robyns, Gwen.
    The potato cookbook.

    Published in 1974 under title: The friendly potato and a cookbook.

    Includes index.

    1. Cookery (Potatoes) 2. Cookery (Sweet potatoes) 3. Potatoes. 4. Sweet potatoes. I. Title.
TX803.P8R6 1976   641.6′5′21   76-43322
ISBN 0-916144-11-9

Contents

Color Illustrations

Dedication

To my husband Paul von Stemann—my favorite Boy Scout cook—whose idea this book was.

To the kind friends who not only ransacked their own recipe books but those of their grandmothers.

To the Potato Board and the Idaho Potato Commission, and to the United States Department of Agriculture and the Potato Marketing Board of England, for their friendliness and positive help.

To Ann Clark, for her patience in unscrambling my thoughts in preparing this manuscript.

To my publisher and friend, Barbara Holdridge, for her joyous enthusiasm.

The Peripatetic Potato

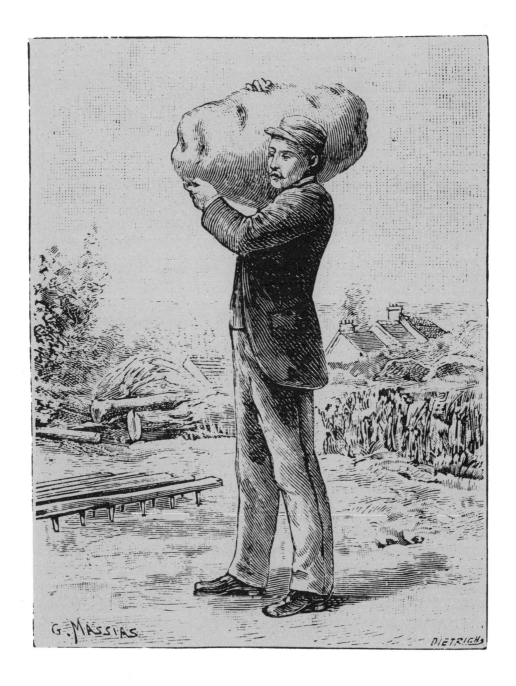

Potatoes have been called "apples of love" because of their aphrodisiac qualities. The Incas battered each other to death so that they could use human blood to fertilize the fields for growing the precious tuber. Marie Antoinette used to wear a sprig of the delicate blue flower in her coiffure. Ben Jonson and Shakespeare wrote exalted words about potatoes. Hitler demanded that a statue of Sir Francis Drake, with a flowering potato in his hand, be torn down at Offenburg. And to this day pious Catholic priests sprinkle Holy Water on the round brown knobs before they are officially planted on Good Friday.

Certainly the potato is the most useful of all vegetables on this earth, easy to grow, cheap, able to be prepared in so many ways, and highly nutritious.

This is not an ordinary cookbook. It is a love story. It tells how to make potatoes into delicious food for all seasons. And it relates the history and romance of the potato; for the small brown tuber has not only captured the imagination of all people of the world, but has changed economic and social structures as has no other vegetable.

Potatoes have many names: papata (Spanish), peruna (Finnish), cartofla (Rumanian), brambor (Czech), panbowka (Polish), kartof (Bulgarian), krtola (Serbian), kartofel (Russian and German), yang shee (Chinese), pomme de terre (the lovely French name), papa (Peruvian) and murphy (Irish). The Scots gave them the repulsive name spud, which was the original name for a digging spade or three-pronged fork. Call it what you may, the potato springs from the plant *Solanum tuberosum esculentum*, the Latin name chosen by the eminent Swiss botanist Gaspard Bauhin.

The early potato originated high up in the grandeur of the Andes of South America, where the air is pure and the sun strong. On the warm lush coastlines manioc and maize were the staple foods, but from 10,000 feet upwards, it was the small brown tubers of the wild solanums that kept the Indians healthy. For this was their staple diet, along with quinoa, whose seed is used like oatmeal, and oca, another tuber-bearing plant.

So sturdy was the original wild strain that some forms were found as high as 15,000 to 16,000 feet; but these bore little resemblance to the cosy, plump potatoes we know today.

The Peruvians not only ate the potato raw but found that if boiled or roasted on hot embers it tasted even better. These advanced people also discovered how to preserve potatoes by a combined freezing and drying method. The potatoes harvested by the women were left on the high plateaus to catch the frost at night. During the day all the family joined in stamping the potatoes, much as the French peasant trod his grapes for wine. The resulting pulp was finally squeezed of all liquid and set out in the sun to dry. This was known as chuno—the "instant mash" of its day.

Inca housewives depended as much on chuno for out-of-season feeding of the family as the harassed working housewife of today depends on dried or frozen foods. When the pre-Columbian graves were opened up lower down on the coast, dried potatoes in perfect condition were found in many of them, much as the Egyptians had stored their wheat in the pyramids.

The Spanish scouting parties of the explorer Gonzalo Jimenez de Quesada, exploring the high plateau surrounding the village of Sorocota in 1536, were probably the first Europeans to discover the potato. As the terrified natives fled, the Spaniards ransacked their houses looking for food. Among the stores of maize and beans were brown balls that looked like truffles. Did they take a bite and spit them out, or did they think they had found a new nut?

It is to the Russians that we owe much of our knowledge of the history of the potato. Led by the eminent geneticist N. I. Vavilov, the Russians spent eight years from 1925 combing the entire South American continent, not only documenting the history, but also making notes on various specimens of the potato. Vavilov produced statistics that confirmed that the potato originated in South America, and was not only unknown in North America but had to be reintroduced there by English colonists, in a second attempt to found the colony of Virginia in the eighteenth century.

The event of the arrival of the potato in Europe is still mysterious. It is fairly safe to assume that it took place in Spain, the only country at the time to have any physical contact with South America. But was it bartered by the friendly natives for pineapples and chickens traded by the crew of Columbus' ship? Is it true that potatoes first arrived in Spain in 1534, brought by a follower of Pizarro? Or did the pious monk Hieronymus Carden bring some tubers back in his habit on his return to Spain in 1570?

It has also been said that Sir John Hawkins brought back some tubers in his ship the "Jesus of Lubeck" from his visit to Sante Fe in Venezuela in 1565, but these are more likely to have been the sweet potatoes, since the potato as we know it was quite unknown in this region at the time.

¶ *The Description.*

VIrginian Potato hath many hollow flexible branches trailing vpon the ground, three square, vneuen, knotted or kneed in sundry places at certaine distances: from the which knots commeth forth one great leafe made of diuers leaues, some smaller, and others greater, set together vpon a fat middle rib by couples, of a swart greene colour tending to rednesse; the whole leafe resembling those of the Winter-Cresses, but much larger; in taste at the first like grasse, but afterward sharp and nipping the tongue. From the bosome of which leaues come forth long round

round slender footstalkes, whereon grow very faire and pleasant floures, made of one entire whole leafe, which is folded or plaited in such strange sort, that it seemes to be a floure made of fiue sundry small leaues, which canot easily be perceiued, except the same be pulled open. The whole floure is of a light purple colour, striped downe the middle of euery fold or welt with a light shew of yellownesse, as if purple and yellow were mixed together. In the middle of the floure thrusteth forth a thicke flat pointall yellow as gold, with a small sharp green pricke or point in the midst thereof. The fruit succeeds the floures, round as a ball, of the bignesse of a little Bullesse or wilde plumme, green at the first, and blacke when it is ripe, wherein is contained small white seed lesser than those of Mustard: the root is thicke, fat, and tuberous, not much differing either in shape, colour, or taste, from the common Potato's, sauing that the roots hereof are not so great nor long, some of them are as round as a ball, some ouall or egge-fashion, some longer, and others shorter; the which knobby roots are fastned vnto the stalks with an infinite number of threddy strings.

¶ *The Place.*

It groweth naturally in America, where it was first discouered, as reporteth *Clusius*, since which time I haue receiued roots hereof from Virginia, otherwise called Norembega, which grow & prosper in my garden as in their owne natiue country.

¶ *The Time.*

The leaues thrust forth of the ground in the beginning of May; the flours bud forth in August, the fruit is ripe in September.

¶ *The Names.*

The Indians call this plant *Pappus*, meaning the roots; by which name also the common Potatoes are called in those Indian countries. Wee haue it's proper name mentioned in the title. Because it hath not only the shape and proportion of Potato's, but also the pleasant taste and vertues of the same, we may call it in English, Potatoes of America or Virginia.

‡ *Clusius* questions whether it be not the *Arachidna* of *Theophrastus*. *Bauhine* hath referred it to the Nightshades, and calls it *Solanum tuberosum esculentum*; and largely figures and describes it in his *Prodromus, pag. 89.* ‡

The

¶ *The Temperature and Vertues.*

The temperature and vertues be referred to the common Potato's, being likewise a food, as also a meat for pleasure, equall in goodnesse and wholesomnesse to the same, being either rosted in the embers, or boiled and eaten with oile, vineger and pepper, or dressed some other way by the hand of a skilfull Cooke.

‡ *Bauhine* saith, That he heard that the vse of these roots was forbidden in Bourgondy (where they call them Indian Artichokes) for that they were persuaded the too frequent vse of them caused the leprosie. ‡

What is known, however, from the account books of the Hospital de la Sangre at Seville, is that potatoes were bought as part of normal housekeeping as early as 1576. The potatoes were bought in units of twenty-five pounds in the fourth quarter of the year, which indicates that they had in fact been grown from tubers brought to Spain, and not imported. They were treated as great luxuries and given to patients as exotic appetizers.

The romanticists give the credit for their introduction to England to the dashing Sir Francis Drake. During his plundering escapades along the coast of Peru in 1578, Drake's cook is said to have taken on stores of the strange tubers at Cartagena in Spain in order to give his men fresh food to ward off scurvy, the sailors' curse. But how could he have known at that time of the valuable vitamin C that lies beneath the thin brown skin? Was it pure guesswork or some strange alchemist's intuition? What was certain is that his crew desperately needed fresh food to keep healthy, and potato goodness could be stored.

Drake left Cartagena on March 30, and after picking up Hariot and the desolate returning English settlers from Virginia, arrived at Plymouth, England, on July 26, 1586. According to A. E. W. Mason in *Life of Drake*, apart from the 110,000 ducats that Drake had won as a ransom for Cartagena, the mission had been a failure. This was due to the fact that he had missed, by a mere twelve hours' sailing, the Spanish Plate Fleet laden with bullion. What irony that in the hold of Drake's ship, unrecognized by the scientist Hariot and the great seaman, lay a fortune more precious than all the gold of the Spanish Main—potatoes.

Drake had long been aware of the potato as a satisfactory food. He had first come across it in the Isle of Mocha off the coast of Chile on November 28, 1577, on his tour around the world. In his journal he wrote:

> *We being on land, the people came down to us to the water side with shew of great curtesie, bringing to us potatoes, rootes and two very fat sheep.*

Of such stuff is history made that school children are reared on the flamboyant fact that Sir Walter Raleigh threw down his cloak for his haughty queen, Elizabeth I. Few of them realize that so many of the new plants that came from the New World were brought back by this eminently cultured scholar. And divers plants they are, ranging from the sweet-smelling yellow wallflower of today's domestic garden, which Raleigh picked up in the Azores, to the glorious potato.

So whether Drake was in fact the first to introduce the potato to England is debatable. But what is established is that Raleigh personally introduced it to Ireland, where he had an estate. In 1699 the botanist John Houghton wrote in his weekly bulletin:

The potato is a bacciferous herb, with esculent roots, bearing winged leaves and a bell flower. This I have been informed was brought first out of Virginia by Sir Walter Raleigh, and he stopping at Ireland, some were planted there, where it thrived well and to good purpose for in three successive wars, when all the corn above ground was destroyed, this supported them; for the soldiers, unless they had dug up all the ground where they grew and almost sifted it could not extirpate them; from whence they were brought to Lancashire, where they are very numerous, and now they begin the spread all the kingdom over.

The first mention in print of the potato comes from John Gerard's catalogue, published in 1596. As barber-surgeon to the Livery Company of the City of London, he kept one of the finest gardens in London, probably situated by Fetter Lane running into Fleet Street. Here this seasoned traveler kept a collection of the most varied plants and herbs he could find. Though Gerard in his book *Herbal* made a mistake in assigning its origin to Virginia, his description of the tubers is decidedly quaint and cogent:

Round as ball, some ovall or egge fashion . . . which knobbie rootes are fastened unto the stalkes with infinite number of threddie strings.

A man of considerable vanity, he was so keen to have his name identified with the arrival of this botanical curiosity that he commissioned his portrait to be painted holding a sprig of the potato plant.

By 1601, according to the French botanist Jules Charles de l'Ecluse, potatoes had arrived on the French dinner table to be eaten with mutton, in the same way as other root vegetables like carrots and turnips. A hypothetical story is that King Philip II paid homage to the Pope in Rome with a gift of the tubers, which bore a resemblance to his name (pappas). Their aphrodisiac qualities were said to be much appreciated by the Pope. One is tempted to wonder why. It is much more likely, however, that the tubers were carried from Spain to Tuscany by no more illustrious a person than a wandering monk. From there the natural stepping stone was Austria, and eventually, according to seventeenth century writings, it appeared in Switzerland and France.

Not every country welcomed the little brown tuber enthusiastically. In Burgundy, for instance, it suffered a set-back when the people of that province were persuaded that "too frequent use of them caused leprosy." In Paris the *beau monde* were torn between improving their powers of love-making or braving the dangers of contracting the dreaded leprosy.

It was not until the French rural economist Antoine-Auguste Parmentier served potatoes from his own garden and persuaded King Louis XVI to wear a potato flower as a button-hole garland, that they were socially accepted. Court banquets soon served up the potato with lavish inventiveness, and French and German chefs vied with each other to produce such creations as Pommes Marguerite and Snow Potatoes with Sour Cream. When Parmentier died, France remembered him with gratitude, and every year potatoes were planted on his grave.

The Russians were highly suspicious of potatoes when they first arrived there in the eighteenth century. Along with cane sugar and tobacco they were thought to be food from the devil. So lurid were the early tales of the potato in Prussia and the legend that it was the cause of scrofula, rickets and consumption, that despite the fact that the citizens of Kolberg in 1774 were starving, they would not touch a tuber. When Frederick the Great sent a wagon load, all the thanks he got was the answer: "The things have neither smell nor taste, not even the dogs will eat them, so what use are they to us?"

Slowly the little brown knobs took over Europe. As the nineteenth century drew to a close, the celebrated Francillon Salad was all the rage in Paris. This was a creation composed of sliced potatoes cooked in bouillon, marinated in champagne, tossed with shallots, herbs and mussels previously poached in wine, then placed delicately in the costliest crystal bowl available, and finally covered with an entire layer of sliced truffles. And in Germany, a hill above the little village of Hirschhorn, in the Neckar Valley, was made the site of a "Potato Monument," with the inscribed dedication, "To God and Francis Drake, who brought to Europe for the everlasting benefit of the poor—the Potato."

Potatoes not only filled hungry bellies but began to obtain immortality by encroaching into folklore. Thus pregnant women lived in fear of eating potatoes at night lest their babies be born with shrunken heads. A peeled potato carried in the pocket was assumed to cure toothache, and a dried potato worn around the neck was considered just the thing to help rheumatism.

In Ireland today, when the housekeeping purse is getting a bit low at the end of the week, they say: "Potato and point." This saying goes back to the early eighteenth century when the Irish peasants' diet was almost exclusively potatoes and buttermilk. Many families tasted meat only on Christmas Day and Easter Sunday. A barrel of 280 pounds of potatoes lasted a week in a family of five. With high rents, no weekly wages and the lack of home industries, food was always scarce. A red herring used to be hung from the beams of the cottages and as the family tucked into their plates of the inevitable boiled potato, the mother would point to the herring, invoking some of its flavor to descend into the plain potatoes. And so the saying "potato and point" was created and became a family colloquialism.

It was in Ireland too that the potato played its most momentous role. Lacking the control of its own destiny—which was in the hands of absentee English landlords—and with crippling trade restrictions, high tariffs on exports of beer, glass, woollen cloth, candles, soap, sail-cloths and linens, Ireland was forced to draw economic strength from its soft rains and black soil. There was nothing else left to its people.

In this despairing climate the humble potato came into its own. It became the savior of Irish husbandry. But even the cultivation of this crop was beset with problems, with the Irish peasant struggling for an existence on his grossly over-rented allotment. In *The History and Social Influence of the Potato*, Redcliffe Salaman aptly sums up the horrifying exploitation of the Irish peasant and significance of the potato:

> *It is of interest to note that it was not the confiscation by enclosure of the relatively few small commons remaining which gave rise to the Whiteboy movement of 1760, but the harshness and chicanery employed in the collection of the tithe on the potato, and the resentment felt in Munster at the conversion of tillage, which included the potato patches of the poor, to grazings. It was not the first time in history in which the potato, as such, made its entry on the political stage but, as in 1728, its role was essentially a social-economic one.*

The failure of the Irish potato crop in 1845 was a tragedy of such alarming proportions that its effect has riccocheted down to many of the present-day Irish troubles. Without warning, a disease called potato

blight swept like a roaring prairie fire throughout the country. Fields filled with promise were reduced to withered, black stalks in forty-eight hours. Before the peasants had time to lift their crops, the tubers were stained like leprosy and beginning to rot. The putrefying stench of the dying fields was nauseating. Nor was the disease localized only in Ireland. In England and Europe it had already been detected and was thought to be linked with dreaded cholera.

That the Irish survived a second year's failure of the potato crop in 1846 at all is one of the great unsolved mysteries. The whole crop, valued at sixteen million pounds, was lost. A writer of the day describes the pitiful scenes:

> *I confess myself unmanned by the extent and intensity of suffering I witnessed, more especially among the women and children, crowds of whom were to be seen scattered over the turnip fields, like a flock of famished crows, devouring the raw turnips, and mostly half naked, shivering in the snow and sleet, uttering exclamations of despair, whilst their children were screaming with hunger.*

Hunger was not the only enemy. A nation that had become dependent on the potato for supplying its daily intake of vitamins now fell prone to scurvy, dysentery and other ills, although the enlightened turned to nettles and wild herbs which they cooked and ate to supplement their diet. In the records of the day two illnesses appeared alarmingly on the increase—ophthalmia leading to blindness caused through the absence of vitamin A, and insanity due to the lack of one of the B vitamins.

The cost of the potato famine in terms of life and health of a nation is still debated to this day. It has been estimated that through death, starvation and emigration, Ireland lost over 2,000,000 of its proud, handsome people. Even more far reaching, the whole history of America —which has given us such illustrious Irish phenomena as the Kennedys and the New York police force—might indeed have been written quite differently.

The Potato in Art

From as early as two thousand years ago the potato has been a theme in art. Its round form was a natural for the Peruvians to translate into applied art, as well as murals. The Inca sculptors, with a wry sense of humor, made potato shapes from clay and turned them into pots in the form of human caricatures. These monstrous potato tubers with grotesque human faces, bulging eyes and cancerous features, became works of art. In some, animal heads were interspersed with human ones sprouting from one large tuber. Many pots, fashioned with immense skill, portrayed a sexual relationship, as if two people were bundled inside a huge potato to make love.

The National Museum in Lima has probably the largest collection of these fascinating potato pots, but the British Museum has at least one superb pot of the Proto-Chimu period. The body of the pot is a tuber with conventionalized painted "eyes." The sides of this head sprout two monkey heads, while yet a third knob is painted like a head which appears to be in sexual relationship with the main figure. Bizarre, powerful, magnetic, it is one of the most splendid examples of these pots in existence today.

The seventeenth-century botanists delighted in making woodcuts of the exciting new find from South America. In Gerard's *Herbal* (1597), Parkinson's *Herbal* (1629), Clusius' *Historia* (1629) and *Jean Bauhin's Historia* (1650) are charming stylized woodcuts of the potato as we know it today, showing the flowers and comical tuber roots.

In seventeenth-century Flemish and Dutch art, when some of the greatest still-life pictures we have were painted, the potato was still virtually unknown in Europe. Instead the painters of the day, like de Heem, captured the new affluence of the Low Countries with canvases depicting great tables laden with exotic fruits—lemons, oranges, melons, strawberries, peaches, grapes and flagons of wine.

It was Vincent van Gogh who gave the potato its status in the world of art. With his compassionate and inquiring mind, he saw in the potato a new relationship between man and the soil. He painted at least four important still-life canvases devoted entirely to the potato. During two years, 1883 and 1884, spent at Neuenen, a flat, marshy part of Holland, he became part of the community, documenting the life of the hard-working peasants. Whether unconsciously or not, the potato became the main theme of most of his peasant studies of this period.

His greatest picture, called simply "The Potato Eaters," was painted in 1885. It shows a family of three peasant women, in their white coifs and cumbersome dresses, a child and a man sitting around a table under a hanging oil lamp. They look carved in wood. In the center is a large dish of steaming potatoes, and one woman pours coffee. Their hands are thickened by work, their backs bowed with fatigue. The clock on the wall says 11:25 p.m. All the agony of that long, despairing day can be seen in the eyes of the man, all the anxiety and hopelessness in the weary face of his wife. Only the child is oblivious of the despair and fatigue.

In a letter to his brother, van Gogh wrote:

I have tried to make it clear how these people eating their potatoes under the lamplight, have dug the earth with those very hands they put in the dish, and so it speaks of manual labor, and how they have honestly earned their food . . . all winter long I have had in the hand the threads of this tissue, and have searched for the definite pattern, and though it has become a tissue of a rough and coarse aspect, nevertheless the threads have been selected carefully and according to a certain rule.

Van Gogh was so drawn to this theme that he painted three different canvases. Two remain in the family today and the third can be seen at the Rijksmuseum Kroller-Muller, Otterlo, in Holland.

In addition to this, van Gogh made many studies of the potato's place in peasant life: the women peeling potatoes, the men digging them, backs bent over harvesting, faces crippled with exhaustion. And always the potato, which had brought life, if not hope, to millions of people throughout Europe.

From Ireland in the first half of the eighteenth century we have some of the most charming pieces of silver ever designed. These are the potato baskets that graced the elegant dinner tables of the landed gentry. Functional, yet extremely delicate, they replaced the wooden bowls of the peasants in the Georgian squares and country houses. The baskets were, in fact, rings which were placed over a white damask napkin. The rings contained the potatoes while the damask absorbed any dampness. All the dish rings seem to have been made in Dublin from the mid-1700s to 1808. The most elaborate, in silver with piercing and repoussé work, are collectors' pieces of great value today. When Sheffield plate rings were made, the elaborate family crests, scrolls and flowers of the silver designers were replaced with graceful symmetrical designs. While the best of these potato rings are to be found in the National Museum in Dublin, the Victoria and Albert Museum also has a small collection.

Potato cauldrons made of cast iron with beautiful, simple shapes are also a relic of Ireland's contribution to potato history. Standing on three legs, these sturdy pots can now be seen in the National Museum in Dublin.

Many of the flat reed baskets that can now be bought in handcraft shops are, in fact, variations of the original potato skibs in which the potato was served in the peasant cottages of Ireland.

Even the Staffordshire works immortalized the potato by making a series of potato pots with open spouts. Opinion is divided today as to whether they were made as gin bottles or were intended to be filled with hot water, stoppered and carried by ladies in their muffs as hot water bottles. The Brighton Museum in England has an amusing collection of these bottles.

The sweet potato even has its place in interior decoration. With its lush green foliage, the sweet potato makes a charming and unusual house plant and is particularly suitable for modern interiors. All you do is to leave a tuber in a warm place to sprout, and then suspend it in water. See that the sprouting roots just reach the water and that the eye is above the water. Soon leaves will appear and grow into a plant. Keep the flowers and berries away from children; they are poisonous.

Potato Types

Pentland Crown

POTATO TYPES

Potato research in America has been supported mainly by the United States Department of Agriculture. Its programs have resulted in potatoes that are highly resistant to plant disease and have flavor and cooking qualities superior to those potatoes that were produced even ten years ago. It's a rather mixed blessing, for it gives too wide a range from which to choose. There are over 80 varieties on the market, and even farmers have difficulty telling them apart. Yet most purchasers are content to buy the first potatoes that catch their eyes. The more attention the shopper pays to buying potatoes, by demanding that they should be named in the shop and not just called "reds" and "whites," the better his or her cooking will be.

Selective buying not only means better cooking, but also ensures that the appearance of the food is improved and menu planning becomes a joy.

A potato's cooking characteristics are determined to a great extent by its starch content. Boiling or "new" potatoes tend to be dry and firm in texture when cooked, since their sugar content has not yet turned to starch. A baking or old potato, with its higher starch content, makes ideal mashed potatoes, light, airy and almost soufflé-like in consistency.

In American supermarkets potatoes are generally packaged as boiling and new potatoes in one category or as baking and old potatoes in another. Despite a study showing that customers would pay higher prices if potatoes were marked as suitable for more specific purposes, little attention is paid to names, and it is up to the self-educated shopper to choose. Here, in essence, is a guide to the wealth of potatoes which should be available.

But remember that buying "bargain" potatoes is false economy. There is far more wastage in damaged, diseased and green potatoes, and in any case they take far longer to prepare. And watch out for dirty potatoes. Potatoes are usually brushed or washed at the point of packing. Dirty potatoes are unsightly, and the dirt itself contributes weight for which you are paying.

NEW POTATOES

These light-skinned potatoes are usually available from January through September, although the term occasionally is used for fall crop potatoes dug before they are fully mature.

New potatoes should be purchased in small quantities, since only recently harvested potatoes have the full, fresh flavor everyone enjoys. If the skins rub off easily, the potatoes are fresh. Use them quickly, and do not store for more than 48 hours. Boiled or lightly sautéed, they are incredible.

FALL CROP POTATOES

Harvested in September or October, these are the staple potatoes we rely on for most of our year-long needs. They are stored for one to nine months before being shipped to the local outlets, and can be stored at home also, in a cool, dark, well-ventilated place. After long storage the red varieties tend to lose their skin colors and identification is extremely difficult.

Temperatures over 50 degrees produce both sprouting and shriveling. No need to throw these out, but be careful to break off the sprouts and peel the potatoes before using. If your potatoes suddenly look green, you have been unkind enough to expose them to light. Since greening produces a bitter flavor (caused by alkaloid Solanin), cut off the entire green area before using the potato.

And, as with Señorita Banana, never put potatoes in the refrigerator. Below 40 degrees, they develop a sweetness resulting from conversion of some of their starch into sugar; and also, with all that sugar, become darker in cooking.

Raw potatoes with blackened areas have been exposed to freezing temperatures.

VARIETIES OF POTATOES

Potatoes bear romantic names—a tribute by their growers, perhaps, to their exotic history. How they trip off the tongue—White Rose, Norgold Russet, La Rouge, Chippewa, Katahdin; and those of the English and Irish cousins as well: Arran Pilot, Red Craigs Royal, Ulster Prince, Désirée, Maris Piper, Pentland Dell.

Unfortunately, to ask for potatoes by variety at the supermarket is to court the manager's blank stare. It's Maine or Eastern or California or Idaho there, with the seasonal new potatoes to refresh the spirit. Here, however, are the true designations, as classified by shape and skin color:

Round White Group

> The regular white to buff or brown color. Best for boiled, roasted, sugared and foiled potatoes, and for salads.

Kennebec (large, elliptical to oblong, skin cream to buff)
Katahdin (principal variety in this group; large, cream to buff)
Superior (earlier and smaller)
Norchip (used mostly for producing potato chips)
Irish Cobbler (medium to large, round)
Monona (fairly new variety)
Sebago (large, elliptical to round)
Ontario (large, oblong, skin dark cream to buff)
Chippewa (large, elliptical to oblong)

Round Red Group

> Naturally red-skinned, and produced, by a happy coincidence, in the Red River Valley of North Dakota and Minnesota. Same uses as Round Whites, but especially superb when boiled, roasted or foiled.

Norland (a somewhat recent introduction, becoming increasingly popular)
Red Pontiac (principal variety in this group; large, oblong to round)
Red La Soda
La Rouge
Red McClure (grown in the Rio Grande Valley in Colorado, and marketed primarily in the Midwest)
Russet Rural

Note: Red potatoes and some white varieties are sometimes treated with colored or clear wax before shipment, to "improve their appearance." The Food and Drug Administration requires that potatoes so treated be plainly marked. And remember that under the Federal Food, Drug, and Cosmetic Act, it is *illegal* to color "white"-skinned potatoes red or to use

colored wax *to make potatoes appear fresher or of better quality.*
Several producing states have banned all use of artificial color. Hope-
fully, more may follow. One tip-off to the presence of artificial color
is the seepage of red into the potato flesh itself. If you can show that the
coloring has in fact penetrated the flesh and causes excessive (more than
5 per cent) waste, return the potatoes to the store from which you
bought them. This is also your recourse if the coloring is unsightly, or
conceals any other defects which cause damage.

Russet Group
> Normally brownish, rough, scaly or netted skin. Best for
> steamed, baked, mashed, sautéed, french fried, fritters, crisps.
> Russet Burbank (long russet). The variety of Idaho potato devel-
> oped by Luther Burbank; now grown widely in other areas as
> well, although three small regions in Idaho still account for
> over 25% of all of America's potato production (which now
> totals nearly 32 billion pounds).
> Norgold Russet (a long to blocky, lightly russeted potato, becoming
> increasingly popular)
> Russet Rural (large, oblong, broad, flattened, dark buff)
> Russet Sebago (not as long as Russet Burbank but longer than
> Russet Rural)

Long White Group
> Thin-skinned, with barely apparent eyes. The closest to all-
> purpose, but not equal to Russets for baking.
> White Rose (the California long potato; skin light cream, large,
> elliptical, slightly flattened)
> Mohawk (large, oblong, medium broad, skin smooth, buff, slightly
> russeted)

GRADING AND PACKAGING OF POTATOES

For even cooking, potatoes prepared together should be uniform in size.
Potatoes are sized mechanically after they are cleaned, and are sorted
into grades by packinghouse workers, according to the potatoes' grade
and size. Most potatoes are marketed under the U.S. No. 1 grade, and
bags of potatoes in retail outlets are often labeled U.S. No. 1. The high-
est grade, however, is U.S. Extra No. 1, for consumers who are in
search of the best. The tolerances for defects are stricter than those for
U.S. No. 1, and potatoes in this grade can only be slightly affected by
internal defects or sprouts. Variation in size within a package is
limited: generally, they must vary by no more than 1¼ inches in
diameter or 6 ounces, with the minimum size being 2¼ inches or 5
ounces. If potatoes are packed under continuous USDA inspection, the
grade name may be shown within the official shield. But grade labeling

is not required by Federal law, even when potatoes have been officially graded. And sometimes packers label their potatoes by grade whether the potatoes were officially graded or not.

Somewhat confusingly, U.S. No. 1 potatoes are also sometimes labeled Size A. These potatoes must be at least 1⅞ inches in diameter, and 40 percent of the potatoes must be 2½ inches in diameter or 6 ounces in weight or larger.

However, to provide for some margin of error in sizing, grading, cleaning and packing, the Consumer and Marketing Service standards do permit a small percentage of offsize or undergrade potatoes in all grades. These tolerances are guided by USDA studies showing how much damage is reasonable because mechanical harvesting and packing practices in themselves cause a certain amount of unavoidable cuts, bruises and other defects.

The standards also set up optional size designations—"Small," "Medium" and "Large," which packers may use. If potatoes are labeled with these size designations, they must be within definite size ranges, with minimums of 1¾ inches for Small, 2¼ inches or 5 ounces for Medium and 3 inches or 10 ounces for Large.

Potatoes are often pre-packaged these days, in bags containing five, ten, fifteen or twenty pounds. This packaging is done either at the packinghouse, at wholesale houses in city terminal markets, or in the central warehouses of retail supermarket chains. The bags generally are polyethylene, open mesh, paper with a mesh or film window, or plain paper. Avoid these last, since they provide no way of inspecting— not to mention sniffing—the potatoes. (The sniff test assures you that the potatoes are not musty or moldy.) The positive virtues of bagging, however, are not to be gainsaid: ease of purchase and less handling en-route to the purchaser's own potato bin. Since potatoes are nearly as delicate as apples, according to the U.S. Department of Agriculture, they can bruise easily at any stage, from the potato combine which harvests them to the consumer who handles them roughly, tossing them about like the traditional "sack of potatoes!"

When all is said and done, however, the most satisfying way of buying potatoes—for me, at least—is to hand-pick them tenderly out of an open bin at the local produce counter, turning them carefully to make sure that there is not a blemish, cut or knobby second-growth on even a single potato in the lot.

Slimming with Potatoes

The value of a food in a diet depends not only on the content of its various nutrients but also on the quantity eaten. The potato is so cheap, easy to grow, blends so well with almost any other food, and can be prepared in so many ways, that people automatically eat relatively large quantities of this vegetable without effort or undue incursion into the budget. The quantities eaten normally mean that, with relatively little addition of fattening calories, the potato supplies us with almost a third of our vitamin C, and useful quantities of several other vitamins and minerals.

Many people who diet find it sheer agony to deprive themselves of starch. They need the bulk that carbohydrates give to prevent that sinking, empty feeling. The answer is not to give up potatoes. To keep a steady weight there must be a balance between the intake of calories and nutrients. Potatoes help provide a properly balanced diet because they do not yield an excessive amount of calories (served boiled or baked) in proportion to the other nutrients they supply.

Comparing calories in other foods, one hundred grams or three and a half ounces of boiled potatoes contain only 80 calories, as against 243 in a similar quantity of bread, 544 in a grilled pork chop, 302 in steak and kidney pie, 497 in chocolate cake, 385 in roast sirloin of beef, 301 in pancakes and 597 in fried bacon.

Because the effect of all diets is not only based on the calorie intake but on the physical activity of the person concerned, people on a potato diet may find that they do not lose weight immediately. It may even take a fortnight before there are any tangible results. I find that if I do not use the word "diet" and never mention it to skeptical friends—"Oh Gwen, not another diet!"—that I get along better. I tell myself that I am on a health junket, purifying my blood from all those sinful side-kicks to modern living. It may be purely a psychological trick but it works for me.

Children, and women having babies, should have one pint of milk a day or else an additional ounce of cheese. But in any case, it is better to check with your doctor before beginning any diet.

THE CRASH POTATO DIET

For the crash potato diet you merely eat half a pound of potatoes boiled, steamed or baked, three times a day, with a small glass of hot milk. Boil, bake or steam the potatoes in their skins, cut them in half and sprinkle with coarse salt and pepper. As an occasional treat you can add two ounces of cottage cheese but nothing else. The idea is not only to cut down on liquids but to benefit from the fact that potatoes are an excellent antidote to body acids. If you suffer from constipation, this may be a problem now, so take a mild vegetable laxative each day.

THE 1200 CALORIE A DAY DIET

This potato diet was devised by the nutrition expert Dilys Wells, and is not painful or too expensive. You can stick to it for a week. The average weight loss for the week can vary between one and a half to two pounds. This in itself is not sensational but unlike many other diets it works simply because it is not difficult to stick to without cheating.

The basic foods allowed are 5 ounces potatoes (which can be served baked, boiled or steamed), 2 ounces bread, ½ pint milk, 1 ounce butter, 2 pieces of fresh fruit or stewed fruit that has been cooked in a synthetic sweetener, and as large an amount of green vegetables as you like, such as cabbage, sprouts, broccoli, cauliflower, lettuce, cucumber, watercress, tomatoes and onions. But no yellow or orange vegetables.

I find that on this diet it is more sensible to keep to a regular pattern of three meals a day rather than five smaller meals. According to the Manual of Nutrition issued by the British Ministry of Agriculture and Fisheries and Food, there is some medical evidence that the number

of meals a day (and, consequently, the amount of food eaten at one time) does influence the pattern of utilization of food by the body; but in the life we lead today the conditions of work and the time taken in traveling will determine the most convenient eating-pattern for each person. There should be no hard and fast rules.

One misconception is that cold food is not equal nutritionally to comforting hot meals. The very word "meal" has come to mean the consumption of food at a table, and more likely to be hot as opposed to a cold snack, although the Oxford dictionary defines it merely as "the customary occasion of taking food." One of the healthiest eighty-year-old women I know, and quite the best looking, is my mother-in-law who lives in Denmark on a diet that mainly consists of rye bread, boiled potatoes, pickled herring, eggs and cheese. I doubt if she has a hot meal once a week.

You can choose from meat, fish and egg dishes where the calorific value does not amount to more than 500 calories for the day. Alcoholic drinks are high in calories and therefore should be avoided. But if you must weaken—and don't we all—then stick to the odd glass of dry white wine or a glass of soda water with a dash of angostura bitters until the water is palest pink.

What is important in dieting is a sensible start to the day. The efficiency of the muscles is lowest in the morning before the first meal of the day, and therefore it is essential to have a good breakfast.

SUNDAY

Breakfast
    4 oz. stewed prunes*
    1 boiled egg

1 thin slice bread and butter
Tea or coffee

Main Meal
    3 oz. roast lamb
    Small portion roast potatoes
    Brussels sprouts

Orange or pear
Coffee

Lunch/Supper
    Tomato juice
    Potato and cheese soufflé

Carrot and apple salad
Tea or coffee

*Indicates where synthetic sweeteners may be used.

MONDAY

Breakfast

Half grapefruit	1 thin slice bread and butter
1 boiled egg	Tea or coffee

Main Meal

3 oz. cold meat	Apple
Baked tomato or green salad	Coffee
5 oz. baked potato	

Lunch/Supper

Welsh rarebit—1 slice buttered toast	1½-2 oz. cheese
	Tea or coffee

TUESDAY

Breakfast

2 thin slices (2 oz.) lean bacon	Thin slice bread and butter
Broiled mushrooms	Tea or coffee

Main Meal

Ham omelet—2 eggs, 1 oz. lean ham	Stewed apricots*
5 oz. baked potato	Coffee
French beans	

Lunch/Supper

2 oz. cheese	Banana
Mixed salad	Tea or coffee

WEDNESDAY

Breakfast

4 oz. broiled kidney	Tea or coffee
1 slice toast and butter	

Main Meal

Broiled lamb chop—6 oz. weighed with bone and skin	Pear
3 oz. potatoes	Coffee
Boiled cabbage	

Lunch/Supper

3 oz. cottage cheese	Orange
Mixed salad	Tea or coffee
2 oz. potato salad, use yogurt instead of mayonnaise	

THURSDAY

Breakfast

2 oz. lean bacon
Broiled tomatoes

Thin slice toast with butter
Tea or coffee

Main Meal

6 oz. beef stew with vegetables
Cabbage
5 oz. jacket-baked potato

Banana
Coffee

Lunch/Supper

2 oz. herring roe with
    diced cucumber and
    watercress salad

Orange
Tea or coffee

FRIDAY

Breakfast

Small glass, 3 fl. oz. orange
    juice
1 scrambled egg

Slice toast with butter
Tea or coffee

Main Meal

4 oz. broiled cod steak
Peas
5 oz. boiled potatoes

Banana
Coffee

Lunch/Supper

3 oz. cold chicken
Salad

Baked apple stuffed with
seedless raisins
Tea or coffee

SATURDAY

Breakfast

Grapefruit juice
3 oz. haddock or kedgeree
(see following explanation)

Tea or coffee

Main Meal

4 oz. liver (oven-baked) or
    minced beef
4 oz. creamed potato
Green vegetable

Apple
Coffee

Lunch/Supper

Potato-deviled chicken
Broiled mushrooms

2 oz. grapes
Tea or coffee

You will note that Saturday's menu includes—as a reward—two extravagantly good dishes. The kedgeree indicated for Saturday breakfast is a mixture of smoked haddock cooked and flaked into perfectly cooked rice, and tossed with lots of butter. I add a well-beaten raw egg at the last moment. Many recipes also have riced hard-boiled eggs in the mixture. It is soft, comforting, wickedly fattening unless you rigidly limit yourself to three ounces, and has been known to produce wind—in fact no modern honeymoon food. Victorian and Edwardian marriages, however, were practically consummated on kedgeree. It was a great favorite with Winston Churchill, and if made correctly is ambrosia.

I once stayed with a sheik in his palace in the desert, staffed with a thousand servants. The prince looked like a cross between Wolman Hunt's picture "Light of the World" and Robert Taylor. In the orange grove in the morning we met for breakfast. There was a posy of orange blossom on my breakfast plate, and beside the toast there was marmalade made from oranges, with transparent blossoms floating in the jelly—like a fragrant honey.

We walked to the surrounding orange and grapefruit trees, a servant with a silver tray and a long stick behind us. I pointed out which fruit I wanted. He hit it and down it fell, to be gathered up by a small serving boy and placed reverently on the silver platter.

After this there was a huge side table covered with food. And there, in pride of place, was kedgeree. It was soggy and awful, but taste it I did, as a pair of beguiling brown eyes watched me. My host, a prince of Kuk (Iraq), had sent to Cairo in his plane for Elizabeth Arden cosmetics for my bathroom and a Mrs. Beeton cookbook for the breakfast. So solemnly we sat and ate a full-scale Victorian breakfast, course after course, beginning with kedgeree.

And that is reason enough for including kedgeree in one sentimental dieter's breakfast.

The potato-deviled chicken starts with chicken curry, enriched with deviled potatoes, made by boiling and ricing the potatoes, and adding to every cupful one tablespoon of sweet brown pickle, salt and cayenne to taste. When cold, they are shaped into round flattened biscuits, ½" thick, and fried gently in hot fat.

Once you have disciplined yourself, it is then easier to go off on these and even more special treats, like the following recipes, made with potatoes.

Potato and Cheese Soufflé

1½ pounds potatoes boiled in their skins and then peeled
⅔ cup grated cheese
2 tablespoons butter
1 teaspoon French mustard
2 tablespoons cream, or skim milk
salt and cayenne pepper to taste
3 eggs, separated

Rice potatoes and beat with cheese, egg yolks, butter, cream, seasonings and mustard. Fold in stiffly beaten whites lightly and pour into a greased soufflé dish. Place on a low shelf and cook in a 400° oven for 30-40 minutes. Do not open the oven door during cooking. Four servings.

Slimmers' Vichyssoise

3 cups cubed potatoes
1½ cups minced onions
4 chicken bouillon cubes
Dash pepper
2 cups water
1 cup evaporated skim milk
2 tablespoons chopped chives

In tightly covered large kettle or Dutch oven, cook potatoes, onions, bouillon cubes and pepper in 2 cups of water for 30 minutes or until potatoes are tender. Purée potatoes and liquid in electric blender, or press through food mill or sieve until smooth. Stir in milk. Chill, and serve topped with chives. Six servings.

Potato Lorraine

1 pound boiled potatoes
3 eggs
½ cup milk
salt and pepper to taste
½ cup finely grated swiss cheese
grated nutmeg
4 tablespoons butter
1 hard-boiled egg, sliced
anchovies (optional)

Slice potatoes so that they overlap in the bottom of an oven-proof dish. Beat eggs, milk and seasoning and pour over potatoes. Cover with cheese and grated nutmeg. Bake until custard sets and garnish with hard-boiled egg and anchovies, if you like the sharp taste. Four servings.

Potato Pizza

Base:
½ cup cooked sieved potatoes
½ teaspoon salt
2 tablespoons melted butter
½ cup self-rising flour
1 tablespoon milk

Topping:
½ pound sliced tomatoes
1 finely chopped onion
½ cup grated parmesan cheese
small can anchovy fillets

Beat butter, salt, potatoes together until creamy. Add flour gradually and finally add milk to form a stiff dough. Roll into an eight-inch round and fry in a greased pan until the underside is slightly brown. Top with rest of ingredients, anchovies and cheese. Brown under a broiler.

Potato Fish Bake

1 pound peeled and sliced
    new potatoes
2 tablespoons butter
¼ pound mushrooms

1 pound any cooked white fish
½ pound sliced tomatoes
2 tablespoons melted butter

Cook potatoes for five to ten minutes in salted water. Sauté mushrooms in butter. Place fish in a lightly greased oven-proof dish. Cover with mushrooms, sliced tomatoes and potatoes. Brush with melted butter and reheat in a 350 degree oven. Four servings.

Cornish Treasure

1½ pounds boiled new potatoes,
     diced
 ½ pound shrimp, peeled and
     deveined
  2 tablespoons butter
2-3 stalks diced celery

4 grated carrots
½ cup yogurt
1 tablespoon mayonnaise
½ cup grated extra-sharp
    cheddar cheese
watercress for garnishing

Melt butter, gently cook shrimp until curled and pink, and add potatoes, celery and carrots. Stir in mayonnaise and yogurt, but do not boil. Pile into an ungreased casserole and sprinkle thickly with grated cheese. Brown under broiler. Four servings.

Bircher Potatoes

8 medium potatoes, unpeeled
1 tablespoon cooking oil

1 teaspoon caraway or dill seed
1 teaspoon salt

Scrub potatoes thoroughly and cut in half lengthwise. Dry with paper towels and paint thickly with oil. Place them on an oiled baking sheet with the cut side down. Sprinkle with salt and caraway or dill seed. Bake in a 350 degree oven for forty minutes. Serve with or without butter. Eight servings.

Curried Potatoes

2 cups cold boiled potatoes
    cut into cubes
2 tablespoons butter
1 small onion, minced

½ cup chicken stock
2 teaspoons lemon juice
¼ tablespoon curry powder
salt and pepper

Cook onion in butter until yellow. Add potatoes and cook until butter is absorbed. Mix stock, lemon juice and seasonings, pour over potatoes, and cook for twenty minutes very slowly until the stock has been absorbed. Four servings.

Veal and Apple Casserole

1 pound lean stewing veal
2 tablespoons flour
2 tablespoons butter
1 chopped onion
1 pound peeled and sliced
    potatoes

1 cup chicken stock
½ pound dessert apples
1 teaspoon sugar
½ cup yogurt

Cut veal into small cubes and rub the flour in. Melt butter in pan and add meat, turning to brown. Add chopped onion and cook a further five minutes, turning all the time. Add potatoes and chicken stock and pour into casserole. Peel apples and slice, arranging them to form a complete hat. Sprinkle with sugar. Cook in 300 degree oven for two hours and just before serving, beat the yogurt, and pour it over. Four servings.

Potato Burgers

1 pound peeled and grated raw
    potatoes
1 pound raw minced beef
1 beaten egg

1 medium onion minced
    very finely
1 teaspoon Worcestershire or
    soy sauce

Grate potatoes and strain off liquid. Dry in a kitchen paper towel. Add rest of the ingredients and form into hamburgers. Fry in pan until cooked, about eight minutes each side. Four servings.

Potato and Tomato Salad

5 medium-sized boiled potatoes
4 peeled tomatoes
½ teaspoon French mustard
1 teaspoon sugar

2 tablespoons yogurt dressing
pinch of salt and paprika to taste
1 teaspoon any chopped fresh
    herbs

Mix dressing with mustard and sugar. Slice tomatoes and potatoes in alternate layers. Add seasonings and pour mixed dressing over them. Chill for an hour before serving. Sprinkle with herbs, such as parsley, dill, tarragon, chives, basil. Six servings.

Spanish Potato Salad

1 clove garlic
2 cups diced boiled potatoes
2 tablespoons chopped green
    pepper or canned red pimiento
¾ cup chopped onion
3 chopped hard-boiled eggs

About 4 tablespoons yogurt
    dressing
½ teaspoon salt
pepper to taste
½ tablespoon chopped chives
    or spring onions

Rub round salad bowl with garlic. Mix diced new potatoes with pimiento, onion, eggs and dressing. Add salt and pepper. Serve on lettuce leaves with a sprinkle of chives or spring onions. Four to six servings.

Jellied Potato Salad

This is a very pretty luncheon dish made in a ring, filled with tomatoes.

½ pound thinly sliced boiled new
   potatoes
2 chopped spring onions
1 teaspoon chopped parsley
1 chopped green pepper
½ cup chopped cucumber
1 cup shredded lettuce

1 teaspoon salt
½ cup yogurt dressing
1 quart aspic prepared to the
   point of setting (follow
   gelatine package directions)
   sliced tomatoes

Mix all the vegetables gently with salt and dressing so that they do not break. Chill a ring-shaped mold and then add prepared aspic to half inch depth. Leave to set. When quite firm, spread vegetables and then gently spoon over them the remaining jelly, which should be of the consistency of thick cream. Chill until hardened. Turn out and fill with tomatoes for color. Six servings.

Slimmers' Sauce

½ cup yogurt
½ cup cottage cheese

chopped herbs
salt and pepper to taste

Whip yogurt and cheese together. Add herbs, salt and pepper. Pile on top of potatoes baked in their jackets.

POTATO WATER DIET

This must be the simplest of all diets and comes from Scandinavia, where people are particularly health-conscious. It is used in one of the leading health clinics. Weight loss differs, of course, with each person, but I lost two pounds in twenty-four hours and felt at least ten years younger.

    People differ in diets. Some prefer to take on a strict day's dieting when they are busy, simply to take their mind off it. Others prefer to stay in bed all day. But in this strict diet you must find your own pattern. It is tough. I make no excuses, but it does have a cleansing effect, especially after a period of eating and drinking too well.

    Wash two pounds of potatoes very thoroughly. Place them in two and a half pints of cold water and bring to the boil. Cook for five or six minutes, no longer—otherwise much of the valuable vitamin C content will be destroyed. This water is your ration for the day. It can be divided up into six cups distributed throughout the day, ending with a cup just before bedtime.

    As in every diet, remember to check with your doctor. But anyone able to take it easy at home could stand two days of it, and end up gloriously lighter and fitter.

Ways of Preparation

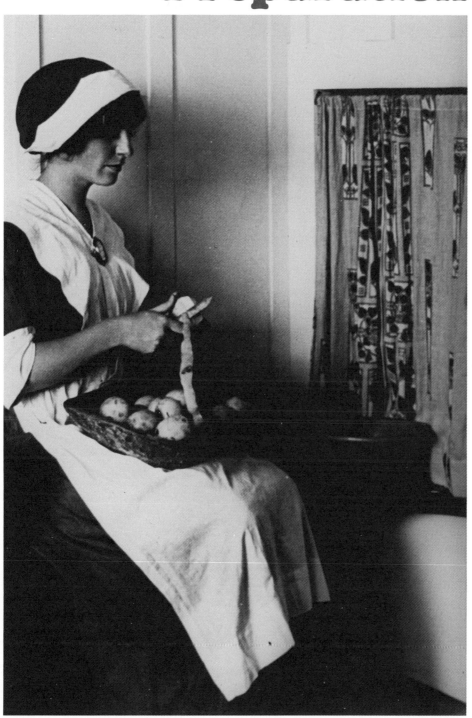

WAYS OF PREPARATION

There are *ten* basic ways of cooking potatoes. Once you have mastered these, the variations are endless. If you are an experienced cook then skip this page. Otherwise ponder on the infinite variety of ways you can use the potato and turn it into glorious food.

Boiling

Cook in only sufficient water to cover, and boil gently before peeling. To seal in the flavor, new potatoes should be plunged directly into boiling water. If potatoes tend to go black when boiling, add a spoonful of vinegar or lemon juice to the water. Remember that potatoes of even size cook better. Use a kitchen needle, sharp skewer or the tip of a vegetable knife for testing. Don't forget to keep the water for soups.

Steaming

By far the best way for mashed potatoes, as more of the goodness and flavor are retained. Cook in steamer before peeling.

Baked Potatoes

Prick with a fork and for appearance's sake coat them with oil to give a shiny jacket. It is worth investing in a potato rack if you have a large family. If not, take care that the potatoes do not touch in the oven or they will go soft. Some people like their potatoes baked with the bottom half covered in foil. This is a pity as half the delight is the contrast between a crisp skin and the mellow soft inside.

Roast Potatoes

Don't forget to roll them in flour before placing them in the oven at 350 degrees in a pan of piping hot fat. Some people parboil them but this is a pity. Long slow roasting in plenty of fat—at least one and a quarter hours—produces a golden, crunchy potato with fat bubbles winking at the brim.

Foiled Potatoes

Scrub twenty-four new potatoes no bigger than a greengage plum. Make a parcel in aluminum foil of the potatoes, a few sprigs of mint or, better still, dill, one ounce of butter and salt to taste. Seal tightly and cook in 350 degree oven for forty-five minutes. As you open the parcel the pungent smell of the potato and herb makes cooking worthwhile.

French Fried Potatoes

After you have peeled and cut the potatoes into lengths, leave for at least half an hour in cold water. This removes the excess starch. Drain and dry in a tea towel or plenty of kitchen paper until quite dry. Fry in a pan one-third full of fat. If this is a family favorite it is well worthwhile investing in a proper deep-frying pot, which is wide, deep and thick-based with a basket to cook the french fries in. For extra crisp potatoes, take a hint from the fish-and-chip shops. Half-cook in fat that is 350 degrees for three minutes (this temperature is reached when a small piece of bread goes brown almost immediately when dropped into the fat). Lift out basket to drain. Turn up heat to 390 degrees and cook french fried potatoes until a deep gold and crisp.

Potato Chips

Once a year it is well worthwhile making your own. It is a long and tedious job but I settle myself with the radio and a bottle of wine and enjoy every minute. Many kitchens now have a meat slicer. I set the blades to thinnest possible, concentrate so that I do not cut my fingers, and make piles and piles. Cook in meticulously clean cooking oil until golden. The slight unevenness of the chips gives them a special kind of charisma. Besides, they taste delicious. Drain well and store in an air-tight tin. They keep for several weeks and only need to be heated in the oven to freshen them up.

Sugared Potatoes

These are especially delicious with pork, duck, goose or ham. For four people you need twenty-four small new potatoes, two ounces butter and six dessertspoons of sugar and two teaspoons salt. Boil scrubbed potatoes until nearly tender. Drain. Melt butter in frying pan and stir in sugar when hot. Blend well and add potatoes, turning them over until they are browned all over. They burn easily so keep fat low once the caramelizing has begun. Sprinkle with salt before serving.

And, of course, there are MASHED POTATOES, FILLED JACKET PO-TATOES and SKILLET POTATOES, deserving chapters to themselves.

Mashed Potatoes

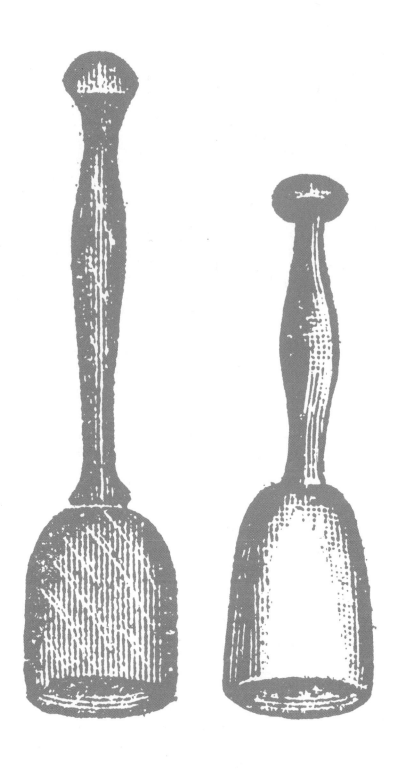

Mashed potatoes are one of the great foods of the world. They rank with caviar, soft-boiled egg, green asparagus, sun-burnished strawberries and that pearl of flesh behind the eye of a boiled cod. But if you want to lift them from a soggy "filler" to become an irresistible point of focus in a meal, they must be treated with respect.

It is a good rule of thumb to work by when cooking, that the cheaper the food the more time and care are required in the preparation, and this goes as much for potatoes as for cheap stewing steak.

For the best flavor and nutriment value, always boil or steam potatoes in their skins and peel while warm. Or alternatively bake in their skins in the oven and scoop out the powdery white flesh when it is soft. When you boil potatoes there is a nutrient loss due to soluble mineral salts and vitamins escaping into the water. The loss of vitamin C in potatoes boiled in their skins is 20–40 per cent, but the loss from peeled potatoes is 30–50 per cent. The cortical layer, which lies just under the skin, is extremely valuable and contains a higher percentage of soluble nitrogenous matter, soluble carbohydrates, minerals and acids than the whole tuber. On the other hand, vitamin C is lower in concentration in the skin than in the tuber itself. The moral of this is never throw away the valuable mineral water in which potatoes have been cooked. Use it for soups, stews and casseroles. And never throw away the skins after you have baked them. Instead, transform them into Potato Skin Treats (page 54).

It is tempting to make mashed potatoes at your convenience and heat them up later. Don't. The loss of vitamin C is greater if they are mashed and kept warm than if kept in their skins and prepared at the last moment.

To give mashed potatoes the right "lift," you will find that sea salt, which you can buy at most grocers or health shops, and freshly ground coarse black pepper are much better than the normal products.

In the following recipes butter is used simply because it gives a richer flavor; but in family cooking margarine can be substituted.

Some of the best mashed potatoes I have ever tasted were in the home of that lovable actress Dame Margaret Rutherford. It was during the period when her husband, Stringer Davis, was doing his "instant guesto" cooking. He was already in his seventies, and as a new cook had no preconceived notions. The chickens were bought off the spit in the shop, the sauce was a tin of concentrated mushroom soup, the beans were deep frozen slivers but the mashed potatoes were divine. They had been treated with loving reverence. Stringer's method was to boil them for twenty minutes exactly and whip with a silver fork, never a potato masher or ricer. He always added warm milk and beat until creamy, but it was not until the end that he popped in a generous lump of cold butter—*never* margarine.

Once in a lifetime I plead with you to indulge in what Alice B. Toklas chose to call "My Extravagant Mashed Potatoes." In the hospitable pre-war atelier in Paris, which this tiny meticulous American lady kept for her close companion Gertrude Stein, it was served to guests like Picasso, Braque, Hemingway. Everyone ate it with the respect it deserved. Of course it is extravagant, but it is worthy of being served as a course on its own. I can assure you it is ambrosia.

Extravagant Mashed Potatoes

4 large floury potatoes   salt and pepper
1 pound butter

Bake the potatoes in the oven for about an hour or until soft, leaving the skins on. Scoop out the white flesh and put through a food mill or ricer. Beat in the butter a little at a time and lastly add salt and pepper. Four extravagant servings.

I enjoy the purity and whiteness of mashed potatoes, but there are many ways of introducing subtle flavors and colors to enrich a meal and delight the eye. I have no quarrel at all with time-pressed cooks who prefer instant mashed potatoes in packs to freshly cooked, but one must acknowledge that they have lost some of their nutritional value in the processing and a great deal of the flavor.

Whether you grow your herbs in a window box or in the garden, fresh thyme, tarragon, dill, parsley, fennel, marjoram, sage, mint, basil, chives and home-grown garlic all add personality to mashed potatoes.

Green Mashed Potatoes

4 large potatoes   1 tablespoon parsley sprigs
½ cup butter   2 tablespoons watercress leaves
1 teaspoon salt   2 tablespoons sweet basil
1 cup light cream   (if you have it)

Bake, steam or boil the potatoes in their skins. Peel and place in a blender at the lowest speed with the rest of the ingredients. When the green has intermingled the potatoes are finished. Serve deliciously creamy. A firmer or softer consistency can be achieved by adding less or more cream.

Mashed Potatoes with Leeks

Proceed as for green mashed potatoes using equal quantities of leeks and potatoes, instead of herbs. Boil the leeks—cut up into one-inch wedges—and peeled potatoes together until soft. Put all through a food mill before adding cream and butter.

Mashed Potatoes with Celeriac

Boil with potatoes equal quantities of celeriac that has been cut into small pieces. When cooked proceed as for ordinary mashed potatoes.

Slimmers' Mashed Potatoes

Use yogurt instead of cream and butter, and add chopped-up parsley and mint to make it look more interesting.

Slim Jim Mashed Potatoes de Luxe

Use yogurt instead of cream and butter, but just before serving whip in the stiffly beaten white of an egg.

Mashed Potatoes with Onions

Add very finely chopped raw onion or sprinkle with chopped spring onions just before serving. The crunchy taste of the onion swimming in its creamy blanket is appealing.

Curried Mashed Potatoes

Add one tablespoon of curry powder to every pound of rich mashed potatoes, and for a more exotic taste sprinkle with slivers of almonds that previously have been roasted brown on a dry pan.

Belgian Mashed Potatoes

Instead of using milk or cream, beat with red "plonk"—a rough Spanish wine is excellent. This is especially good with pork sausages, roast pork or duckling. For every pound of potatoes use one cup of wine.

Irish Mashed Potatoes

I claim to have invented this recipe myself, but I cannot believe that some astute Irish cook did not find it before me. Use Guinness or stout instead of milk. Particularly good with a rich beef stew or goulash. This is strictly a "guests' special" since most children dislike the beery flavor.

Bengal Mashed Potatoes

I first tasted this with some scrawny old chicken in India. The chicken was disgusting but the potatoes were fascinating, and I now serve it in my Oxfordshire farmhouse with any kind of cold meat. Add to two cups of mashed potatoes, ½ cup of rich, dark chutney. Whizz with a fork, pile into a dish and lightly brown under the broiler.

German Mashed Potatoes with Apples

This is a specialty from Thuringen and is a good partner for all pork dishes, fried liver and bacon or sausages. The classical recipe has no salt to dim the fresh apple flavor, but if your taste buds are blunted add salt to taste. Tart cooking apples are best.

1 pound potatoes	1 cup milk
1 pound apples	4 tablespoons butter, divided
	crisp breadcrumbs

Cook peeled apples in half the butter until soft, but be careful not to burn. Boil or steam potatoes in their skins, and when cooked peel them while still hot. Mix both together and if you have the time or patience put the mixture through a food mill. Stir in the milk until the mixture is like thick porridge and add the cold butter at the end. Just before serving sprinkle with the breadcrumbs. Four servings.

Danish Potatoes and Apple Purée

This is the Danish version of the previous German recipe. It is less sophisticated and may appeal to children more, though I personally prefer the fresh taste of the German one.

½ cup butter	2 tablespoons sugar
2 cups hot mashed potatoes	½ teaspoon nutmeg
2 cups unsweetened apple sauce	salt to taste

Beat apple sauce into ordinary mashed potatoes. Add butter and seasoning. Place in a baking dish and swirl into peaks. Bake in a hot oven for thirty minutes until the tops are lightly browned like the Himalayas at dawn. Four servings.

Spanish Mashed Potatoes

I have friends, Josephine and Wyndham Gooden, who have a house in Spain. There are so many things to delight our senses when we arrive —but not the least are the cook Maria's mashed potatoes. She serves them with bland meats such as chicken and veal, as their rosy color takes away the naked look of the meat and adds a piquant taste. If two whipped egg whites are added to the following recipes, they can be piped as meringues and baked till firm. They look like pale pink cumulus clouds.

2 pounds potatoes	2 cloves garlic
2 pounds tomatoes	pepper and salt

Boil potatoes in their skin, peel and mash. Grate tomatoes on a cheese grater to avoid the skin, or peel by dipping in boiling water to loosen the skin. Stew the tomatoes, garlic, salt and pepper until tender. Add to potatoes and spin in a blender or pass through a food mill. The end product should be flamingo pink mashed potatoes that are fluffy and garlicky and look gorgeous. Eight servings.

Hasty Spanish Mashed Potatoes

In the winter I have my own version which, though not quite as delicious, is quick to make in a guest-emergency.

2 pounds potatoes
2 pound can of tomatoes
knob of butter

salt and pepper
garlic

Boil and skin potatoes, add can of tomatoes and seasoning and put in blender or beat well by hand. Eight servings.

Portuguese Mashed Potatoes

A Portuguese version of this, which I first tasted in the home of Tore and Vagn Christiensen in the Algarve district, is less colorful but also has a fresh intriguing taste.

2 pounds potatoes
4 canned pimientos

½ green pepper
pepper and salt

Boil potatoes in their skin, peel and mash with a knob of butter. Add pimientos, peppers cut in small dice and seasoning and beat until fluffy. Eight servings.

Basque Potatoes

The Basques are a proud people, and here is a dish to bring on proudly, in your richest country serving bowl, with its magnificent aroma going on before.

4 cups hot mashed potatoes,
    well seasoned
3 tablespoons olive oil
1 large garlic clove, crushed
1 green pepper, cut in thin strips
2 medium onions, cut in wedges
3 medium tomatoes cut in
    wedges

⅓ cup stuffed olives or pitted
    black olives
1 strip orange peel
½ teaspoon basil
¾ cup dry white wine
Salt and pepper
Chopped parsley

In a large skillet over medium heat, saute garlic, green pepper and onions in olive oil, stirring 5 minutes. Add tomatoes, olives, orange peel and basil; stir in wine. Simmer, uncovered, stirring occasionally, 5 minutes more or until vegetables are tender-crisp. Be careful not to overcook them. Remove orange peel. Season to taste with salt and pepper. Pile mashed potatoes in shallow serving bowl. Spoon vegetables and juices over them. Sprinkle with parsley. Eight servings.

Mashed Potatoes with Cheese

There are endless permutations of this French way of serving mashed potatoes. The main thing is to keep the mashed potato rich and as creamy as porridge before topping with cheese. Though a thin slice of Swiss cheese like gruyére or emmenthal gives more flavor and texture, I frequently use up the last of the "mousetrap" by grating on top. Though parmesan gives a piquant flavor, it dries up if placed under the broiler and is better stirred into the mashed potato. If using parmesan as a topping, dot with butter. This may be done in a large oven-proof serving dish or in individual cocotte pots.

Duchesse Potatoes

One of the favorite classical French vegetable dishes is duchesse potatoes. It can either be used as a piping on a dish such as Coquilles Saint Jacques (scallops in white wine sauce), or shaped into fancy shapes and baked in the oven, or made into patties and fried in butter. The secret is a hot oven, so they brown quickly and do not dry out inside.

2 pounds potatoes	2 eggs (or 4 yolks)
½ cup butter	salt and pepper to taste

Boil the potatoes till soft, and peel. Stir into them the eggs and butter and beat vigorously. In this case, a blender or rotary beater does improve the texture. The mixture is now ready for use.

Potato and Cheese Clouds

1 pound mashed potatoes	salt and pepper
4 tablespoons butter	4 tablespoons grated cheese with
1 large egg, separated	a good strong flavor

Beat the butter and egg yolk thoroughly into the mashed potato, add seasoning and cheese. Whip the white until it stands in peaks and fold into the potato mixture with a feather touch. Place in mounds on a greased baking tray and cook until golden brown in a hot oven. Four servings.

Pomme Fondante

Pomme Fondante is another truly delicious way of preparing mashed potatoes even if it is a once-a-year specialty. Add to two pounds of mashed potatoes one cup of heavy cream, pour into a soufflé dish and sprinkle with one half cup of coarse, stale breadcrumbs. Bake in a hot oven until crumbs are brown. Eight servings.

Potatoes with Sour Cream (Poland)

Poland is one of the big potato-eating nations of the world, and one of the most delicious Polish recipes uses sour cream. The dish is said to have been a favorite of Lord Byron, who claimed it inspired his poetry.

1 pound potatoes
4 tablespoons butter
salt and pepper

1 tablespoon chives
⅔ cup sour cream

Boil potatoes until soft and peel. Put through a ricer or use a fine masher. Whip in the chives and sour cream, and serve immediately. Four servings.

North of England Mashed Potatoes

This is a comforting vegetable for fried sausages or mutton chops.

1 pound mashed potatoes
1 pound cabbage, shredded and boiled
1 large onion, chopped and boiled

4 tablespoons butter, cut into pieces
salt and pepper
¼ pound cheese, grated

Mix the potatoes, cabbage, onion, butter, salt and pepper together and place in a greased oven-proof dish. Sprinkle with the cheese. Heat thoroughly in a hot oven until cheese is browned on top. Six servings.

Provençale Mashed Potatoes

Add to regular mashed potatoes as much canned tomato purée as desired. I prefer mine to be quite strong and also add 1 teaspoon of paprika. Pipe onto a tray like meringues and bake in a hot oven until firm.

Purée of Potatoes and Jerusalem Artichokes

1 pound potatoes
1 pound Jerusalem artichokes
milk

salt and pepper
breadcrumbs
3 tablespoons butter

Boil both vegetables. When soft, peel and put through a food mill. Add sufficient milk to make into a creamy purée and season to taste. Put the mixture into a buttered baking dish, sprinkle with breadcrumbs and dot with butter. Brown in a hot oven. Four servings.

Potato Dumplings

Potatoes are the one vegetable that you can give everyone, and most truthful people will admit to loving them. As Gertrude Stein might have said, "A pea is a pea is a pea," but potatoes have a chameleon character. They can be as delicate as a morning cloud or as robust as a Russian winter. It is simply the way you treat them. On a cold winter's night I love to come home to potato dumplings served with a good old-fashioned beef stew.

1 pound potatoes	fresh chopped parsley or one
1 egg	teaspoon of thyme to taste
½ cup self-rising flour	1 teaspoon baking powder
finely chopped onion	(optional)

Boil potatoes until soft. Peel and put through a potato ricer or food mill to break down the consistency. Add rest of the ingredients and mix well. Form into small balls the size of a walnut. Half an hour before the stew is finished sprinkle the potato dumplings over the top.

Porcupines

Prepare a duchesse mixture of potatoes. Form into balls the size of a tangerine. Dip in a slightly beaten egg and roll in cornflakes or toasted almonds. Deep fry until golden brown. They make delicate "party food" served with fried chicken, mixed grill or escalope of veal.

Mashed Potatoes with Rutabagas

The slightly sweet taste makes this an excellent foil for boiled mutton or boiled brisket of beef. Boil equal quantities of rutabagas and potatoes. To every pound of vegetables add ½ cup of butter. Sprinkle with grated nutmeg before serving.

Cook's Paradise

1 package instant mashed potatoes	1 can condensed mushroom soup

These creamy mashed potatoes can be made in the time it takes a greedy guest to drink a glass of sherry. Instead of using hot milk, substitute the same amount of hot mushroom soup and whip in the usual way. Four servings.

Potato Pudding

This recipe may sound a little fussy but it is well worth the effort.

1½ pounds of potatoes
3 eggs, separated
4 tablespoons butter
salt and pepper to taste

1 tablespoon chopped parsley,
or ½ teaspoon of either
thyme, tarragon or marjoram

Boil potatoes in skin until soft, peel and mash. Add egg yolks, melted butter, herb and seasoning. Whip vigorously until light. Gently fold in stiffly beaten egg whites. Pour into greased bowl, cover with foil, and steam on a rack in a covered pot, in 1½ inches of water, or in a bain marie (water bath) for an hour. Serve with a mushroom or tomato sauce poured over the pudding.

The Potato
in Its Jacket -
the Complete Meal

Some of the most splendid potatoes in the world are grown on the great rolling plains of Idaho in the American Midwest. Here is the perfect soil for growing potatoes of even size and quality. Year after year, as a result of the climate and rich volcanic soil, the potato crop seldom differs—huge, floury potatoes of even size. It was this potato, baked in its jacket, that became the favorite of new settlers, who made history and found a paradise there after crossing from the Eastern seaboard. In England, by contrast, no two fields produce potatoes of like shape or quality.

The settlers' barbecue cooking style had infiltrated from the Caribbean, where whole hogs were split from "beard to tail" and roasted on a gridiron—or a "barbacoa." When the embers had died down potatoes were heaped into the ashes and baked in their jackets. The style became a part of Middle West life—the barbecue and the barn dance were the local marriage markets.

In New Zealand, when I was a child, on high days and holidays, we borrowed the same style of cooking from the Maoris. How many black-charcoaled potatoes and sausages, with raw insides, I have eaten around a bonfire on the beach, saying to myself: "This is living!" Fortunately, the nutritionists now have persuaded us to eat the jackets, and the Idaho potato has adapted to the electric or gas oven. For the best results, choose mature potatoes weighing at least half a pound apiece. Shape is important and there should be no blemishes on the skin. Scrub impeccably clean and dry with a cloth. Rub the potato all over with cooking oil and then make a large cross-shaped incision on the topside.

Some people, including the best American hotels, wrap the base of the potatoes in foil. I can see no virtue in this. I like the skin of my potatoes to be crisp in contrast to a feather-bed soft inside. Place the potatoes in a hot oven and expect that they will take one hour to cook. You can tell when they are done by holding them with an oven mitt and squeezing them gently. When they yield nicely they are done.

Whenever the Duchess of Bedford wants to spoil her husband, when they are staying at her ski chalet at Meribel in the French Alps, she makes him what must be the most de luxe jacket potato in the world. When the potato is cooked, she slits the top and mixes the inside with thick sour cream and chives, chopped hard boiled eggs and a touch of shallot. Just before serving, she adds a large spoonful of caviar. A practical French woman, the duchess also suggests that cod's roe and chopped salmon, instead of the caviar, are just as good!

Within a stone's throw of another ducal palace, Blenheim, England, is a small inn nestling in Park Lane, Woodstock, Oxford. It is called "The King's Head" and dates back to 1735. In 1972 a vital young couple moved in as landlords—Helen and Brian Rendle. They both have degrees in catering, and experience in one of England's most successful chains of commercial inns. But they wanted to be different. They longed to get away from the eternal "sandwiches, pork pies, hot sausages" image. With immense courage, little money and enormous imagination they decided that potatoes in their jackets, piled high with delicious fillings, would be the main food they served. Today the inn is packed to the doors and their customers consume one ton a week.

The Rendles' success is not only that they have hit on a bright idea but that the potatoes, bought in Dorchester, are enormous. They then pay extra to have them specially graded. Beyond this, there is a most generous helping of the twenty-one fillings they supply, and it is all served in the most impeccable and attractive way in wooden bowls. They cook their potatoes by microwave for from four to five minutes and then put them in an ordinary gas oven for 45 minutes to "crisp up."

Try these fillings for jacket potatoes, and serve with a green salad. Here are the fillings the Rendles provide:

Chicken and Curry Sauce
Chicken and Tomato
Chopped Chicken and White
  Sauce
Sweet Corn and Chopped
  Egg
Sweet Corn and Ham
Sweet Corn and Chicken
Curry Sauce and Tomatoes
Baked Beans and Ham
Prawns in Cocktail Sauce
Savoury Mince

Baked Beans
Chopped Bacon and Egg
Bacon and Tomato
Bacon, Egg and Tomato
Bacon and Onions
Cheese, Onions and Tomato
Cheese and Tomato
Chopped Ham and Egg
Cheese and Ham
Cheese and Pickle
Prawns and Curry Sauce

At Christmas the potato comes into its glory with a special turkey-in-cheese-sauce filling.

POTATO SKIN TREATS

And here is my way of using even the potato skin so that (unlike the squeal of the pig), it too can be converted into something not merely edible, but crisply delicious.

Bake potatoes as described on page 40. When they are done, cut each potato in half lengthwise, separating the halves completely. Scoop out all of the contents cleanly, saving them to make any of the recipes for mashed potatoes. Brush the shells inside and out with melted butter, sprinkle them with coarse salt and place them on a rack in the oven, preheated to 350°. Bake them for about twenty minutes, until they are very brown and crisp, and serve them while they are still warm.

Skillet Potatoes

Cooking is like making love. The more you revel in it the more enjoyable it becomes.

When we moved into Holly Court Farm in Oxfordshire, it was not the tiny twelfth-century chapel that tugged at my heart nor the glorious robust beams giving this house of fourteen rooms its ancient elegance. It was not even the large sprawling garden, dizzy with old-fashioned species roses.

It was the large four-oven Aga cooker belching out warmth and friendliness in the large stone kitchen, where once monks had eaten their frugal repast. It was then called Holy Court, and the monks' bread oven still remains as a reminder of its past.

I saw myself standing at that Aga presiding over the hot plates and ovens like one of the great chefs of the past. Like Carrême who ruled his stoves, in the kitchen of the Royal Pavilion in Brighton, with authority and nobility. He invented caramel. What dish could I create that belonged to me alone, but could be shared with friends?

There and then I decided that I would fill the kitchen with wondrous scent of fresh herbs, wine bubbling in sauces and the joyous smell of butter sizzling in a skillet.

So here to share are my favorite potato skillet recipes, all cooked and eaten in my kitchen.

Hopel-Popel

1 pound boiled potatoes, diced
½ cup mushrooms, sliced
4 ounces streaky bacon, diced
1 medium onion, peeled and finely chopped
4 large eggs
¼ cup cheese, grated

Prepare potatoes, mushrooms and bacon. Fry mushrooms and bacon with the onions, gently, then add the potatoes and allow to warm through. Beat the eggs, pour over the potato mixture, sprinkle with grated cheese and cook slowly until the eggs are set. Brown the top under the broiler if necessary. Cut into wedges and serve piping hot. Four servings.

Pan Haggerty

2 pounds potatoes, boiled, peeled and sliced
1 pound onions peeled and sliced
sausages (optional)
4 ounces grated cheese (any mousetrap sort will do)

Place potatoes and onions in a frying pan in layers and finish with optional sliced sausages and cheese. Cover pan with a lid and cook for about twenty minutes or until soft. Just before serving, place under the broiler until cheese bubbles. Four servings.

Potato Yahni

1½ pounds potatoes, peeled
1 cup onions, peeled and
  chopped
2 cloves garlic, peeled and
  crushed
4 tablespoons olive oil

4 tomatoes, peeled, seeded and
  chopped
2 teaspoons sugar
bayleaf, optional
salt and pepper

Cut potatoes into uniform size. Fry onions and garlic in olive oil with potatoes for 2-3 minutes. Add tomatoes, sugar, bayleaf, salt and pepper. Cover and simmer until potatoes are soft. Serve straight from the pot. Four servings.

Egg Domino

2 pounds potatoes, peeled and
  diced
1 large onion, peeled and sliced
4 slices streaky bacon, diced

½ cup milk
2 tablespoons butter
8 eggs
salt and pepper

Prepare potatoes, onion and bacon; butter a large ovenproof dish. Place a layer of potatoes in bottom of dish and cover with half the onion, bacon, salt and pepper. Repeat these layers again, finishing with a layer of potato, salt and pepper. Pour milk over all, dot with butter, cover tightly with aluminum foil and bake for one hour. Remove from oven, make 8 hollows in the potatoes and break in eggs. Return to oven for 10 minutes, until eggs are just set. Serve at once. Four servings.

Sauté Potatoes

The whole of Eastern Europe has survived on these for centuries. Boil for ten minutes, skin and cut in slices. Use bacon fat or butter for the best results—you will need four tablespoons to every pound of potatoes—and cook on a brisk heat. This is a case when you take your drink to the stove so that you can watch them all the time. The result is gorgeous. They should be soft inside and crisp outside.

Potato Fritters

These are really potato pancakes and make an excellent supper dish.

2 pounds potatoes
2 beaten eggs
2 tablespoons flour

1 teaspoon salt
grated nutmeg and pepper
  to taste

Put the potato through the mincer or use a grater. If it goes brown it does not matter as this is camouflaged in the frying. Mix all ingredients together and pour into a greased pan just as you make an ordinary pancake. Cook for about ten minutes until underside is browned. Turn over and cook the other side. It must be thin, crisp and piping hot. It is better to keep two pans going at one time. Four servings.

Browned Potatoes

Use tiny, whole new potatoes. Cook in shallow fat, turning often until golden brown and crisp.

Corn Tricks

2 large potatoes, peeled	8 ounce can sweet corn kernels
4 tablespoons flour	2 tablespoons milk
2 eggs, beaten	butter or oil for frying

Grate the raw potatoes, pour off surplus water, and add flour, beaten eggs, corn and milk. Fry tablespoonfuls until golden, turning halfway through.

Potatoes Sablées

These "sandy" potatoes, as their name betrays, are cut in dice when raw, then fried slowly in butter, some fine breadcrumbs being added towards the end.

Sweet Brown Potatoes

Use tiny, whole, new potatoes. Turn them in syrup (1 ounce butter and 1 ounce sugar) in a frying pan until browned.

Tartan Crispots

Use tiny, whole, new potatoes. After boiling toss in melted butter and then oatmeal flakes. Fry till crisp.

Potato-Carrot Cakes

1 large potato	1 teaspoon salt
4 medium carrots	1/8 teaspoon pepper
1 tablespoon grated onion	1/4 teaspoon tarragon
2 tablespoons flour	4 eggs, slightly beaten
2 tablespoons wheat germ	2 tablespoons butter, divided
3 tablespoons chopped parsley	

Shred potato and carrots on coarse grater. In large bowl combine potato, carrots and onion. Sprinkle with flour and toss to mix well. Stir in remaining ingredients except butter. Melt 1 tablespoon butter in large skillet. Use 1/4 cup mixture for each pancake, spoon onto skillet and flatten, cook 5 minutes, turn and cook 5 minutes longer, or until golden brown. Repeat with remaining mixture, adding remaining butter as needed. Six servings.

Old-Fashioned Potato Patties

2 slices bacon
3 cups cold mashed potatoes
1 egg yolk
2 green onions, sliced

salt and pepper
Tabasco (optional)
bacon fat

Fry bacon until crisp; drain on paper towels; crumble. Reserve bacon drippings. In a large bowl, mix potatoes, egg yolk, green onions and bacon. Season to taste with salt, pepper and Tabasco. Form into 6 patties, 1 inch thick. In a large skillet over medium heat, brown patties on one side in 1 tablespoon fat. With a pancake turner, turn carefully and brown slowly on the second side, adding more bacon fat, if necessary. Serve at once. Six servings.

Chicken and Oyster Hash

1 pound potatoes, cooked and
  peeled
1 cup left-over cooked chicken,
  cubed
1 cup oysters, cut in halves
1 medium onion, diced
6 tablespoons butter, divided

1 teaspoon salt
½ teaspoon pepper, freshly
  ground
½ cup heavy cream
1 lemon's worth of juice
parsley, chopped

Dice the potatoes, and mix them with the chicken and oysters. Sauté the onion in 2 tablespoons butter, add 2 more tablespoons butter, let it melt, and then add the potato mixture, with the salt and pepper. With a wooden spoon, combine all ingredients in the pan. In another skillet, heat 2 tablespoons butter, swirl so that the bottom is well coated, and add the cooked mixture, flattening it evenly in the pan, gently. Cook without stirring, just until the bottom is brown. Then dribble the cream over it, and continue cooking just until the cream is absorbed. Sprinkle with the lemon juice and parsley, and serve with individual lemon wedges. Four servings.

Boxty

1 egg
1 cup buttermilk
2 tablespoons melted butter
½ cup mashed potatoes

1 cup finely grated raw potato
¾ cup sifted flour
1 teaspoon salt
1 teaspoon baking soda

Beat the egg, buttermilk, butter and both kinds of potatoes in a bowl. Sift together dry ingredients and add to liquid mixture, stirring only lightly. Batter will be lumpy. Drop by spoonfuls onto hot greased skillet, and bake as for pancakes. Serve at once, with slices of corned beef, mustard and horseradish accompaniment, as the Irish country folk do. Four servings.

The Breakfast Potato

The potato is the only vegetable that can be eaten around the clock, 365 days in the year. It is doubtful whether anyone could wake up to face even the tenderest asparagus every day of his life, yet millions of people around the world eat potatoes every day, and enjoy them.

Potatoes can form the basis of a nourishing and healthy breakfast, replacing expensive eggs, bacon, sausages and tomatoes. The organized cook can make most of the recipes the night before when he or she is preparing dinner or supper, and merely do the last-minute heating up or cooking in the morning.

Potato omelette takes not much more time to make than listening to the weather report on the radio.

Potato Omelette

4 tablespoons butter
½ cup sieved cooked potatoes
  or cooked diced potatoes
1 tablespoon ketchup
  (optional)

salt and pepper
2 eggs
1 tablespoon cold water
parsley or fried bacon
crumbs for garnishing

Prepare filling by heating potatoes in the omelette pan with the butter and ketchup, taking care that you spread the potato evenly. Add salt and pepper. Beat eggs in a bowl until well mixed but not frothy. Add one tablespoon cold water. Pour over potatoes. Cook as a normal omelette and when the bottom is set and the center still slightly gooey, sprinkle with bacon or parsley and slide off on to a hot plate and fold. Serve really hot. If you want to make it taste even more interesting, add a tablespoon of tomato ketchup. Two servings.

Potato and Corn Drops

3 cups mashed potatoes
½ cup hot milk
2 eggs

salt and pepper to taste
1 small can whole sweet
  corn (optional)
butter for frying

Beat all ingredients together until you achieve a thick batter. Drop by the tablespoon into melted butter. Cook one side until brown, then flick each one over and cook the other side. Six servings.

Sausage Special

1 pound cooked and sliced
   potatoes
4 slices streaky
   bacon
½ pound skinless pork
   sausage, halved

1 cooking apple, peeled
   and sliced
2 eggs
½ cup milk
salt and pepper
1 teaspoon paprika

Cook bacon for five minutes in dry pan until the fat melts. Push to one side and fry sausages and apple slices. Line oven-proof dish with potatoes. Place bacon, apples and sausages carefully on top. Beat eggs, milk, paprika, salt and pepper and pour over. Bake for half an hour in a 350 degree oven. This can be made the day before and covered with foil to heat up in the oven while you are dressing in the morning. Four servings.

Potato Frikadeller

Frikadeller is the Scandinavian version of rissole. It is usually made from a mixture of pork meat and veal but is warming when made from potatoes as a breakfast dish.

1 pound peeled and grated
   potatoes
½ pound raw minced meat
1 egg

1 teaspoon tomato ketchup
1 medium onion, chopped
   finely
salt and pepper
butter for frying

Potatoes can be prepared the night before and left in cold water overnight. Dry thoroughly just before using and mix with minced meat, egg, tomato ketchup, chopped onion and salt and pepper. Drop mixture by tablespoon into melted butter in frying pan. When brown, turn over and fry the other side. Four servings.

Potato Club Sandwiches

These are a wonderful treat as a Sunday morning "brunch" during the winter.

1 pound mashed potatoes
4 tablespoons flour
salt and pepper

4 slices bacon
4 eggs
butter for frying

Mix mashed potatoes with flour, salt and pepper. Roll out until a quarter of an inch thick and cut into eight rounds. Fry on both sides until golden. Fry bacon and then eggs lightly on both sides. Place between two potato cakes. Four servings.

Kipper Cakes

These can easily be prepared the day before, all ready for frying.

1 quart boiling water
1 pound kipper or smoked
  mackerel fillets
1 pound mashed potatoes
2 hard-boiled eggs, chopped
chopped parsley
4 tablespoons melted butter
salt and pepper
beaten egg
breadcrumbs
fat for frying

Place kipper or smoked mackerel in a jug and pour over them the boiling water. Blanch for five minutes. Skin and flake fish off bone. Mix together fish and mashed potatoes, hard-boiled eggs, parsley, melted butter and salt and pepper. Pat flat and cut out small circles with a sherry glass or large cookie cutter. Dip in beaten egg, coat with breadcrumbs and fry in shallow fat. Four servings.

Crispy Herrings

The idea is the same as the Scottish herring in oatmeal but much more delicate and fun.

4 herrings
2 eggs
1 large bag potato chips
oil for frying

Clean herrings, cutting off the head and tail. With your thumb run down under back-bone, lifting it out like a zip fastener. The fish will now be flat. Dip in egg beaten with 1 teaspoon of cold water and roll in crushed potato chips. Fry in oil until crispy and turn over to the other side. Four servings.

Sunday Sweet Corn

This evolved from a favorite Sunday breakfast I used to make. The base was smoked haddock but as fish has become more expensive I now make it with mashed potatoes. This can be cooked and kept hot, covered with foil.

1 pound potatoes, seasoned
  and mashed with rich additions
  of butter and milk
1 large can creamed sweet corn
4 eggs
butter for frying

Line an ovenproof dish with hot mashed potatoes. Heat sweet corn and pour it over. Top with eggs that have been fried in butter. Four servings.

Baked Bean Specials

duchesse potatoes, made as
   described on page 48
4 eggs
1 large can baked beans

Pipe the potatoes onto a greased baking tin in the form of small nests. Break an egg into each nest. Cover with baked beans and place in 400 degree oven for fifteen to twenty minutes. Four servings.

Potato Rolls

Potato short pastry, made
   as directed on page 108
¼ pound streaky bacon
2 hard-boiled eggs, chopped
½ cup boiled, diced potatoes
parsley
salt and pepper
milk

Cut streaky bacon into small squares and cook lightly. Toss in potatoes, hard-boiled eggs, parsley, salt and pepper. Roll out pastry and cut into long rectangles. Fill each center with a spoonful of the mixture. Carefully roll up each rectangle, seal edges with cold water, brush tops with milk and bake in 400 degree oven until the pastry is golden (about twenty minutes). Can easily be reheated if made the day before.

Banana and Potato Pancakes

½ cup mashed potatoes
¼ cup plain flour
salt and pepper
1 egg
1 cup milk
oil for frying
2 large bananas
2 tablespoons butter
4 slices bacon

Mix potatoes, flour and salt and pepper. Make a well and drop in the egg. Stir and slowly add milk to give a pancake batter. Fry four pancakes in oil in normal fashion. Stack on plate. Meanwhile, fry bacon until crisp. Pour off fat. Cut each banana in half across the middle (not lengthwise). Gently fry bananas in butter. Roll the bananas in the pancakes. Place in oven to keep hot and top with bacon strips. Four servings.

The Potato
for Luncheon

As a catalyst to left-overs, there is nothing to beat the potato in its lunchtime form. Just a few bits of this and that, and the friendly potato does the rest. A green salad is all you need to give color and variety.

Mushroom Quickie

¼ pound streaky bacon
1 onion, chopped
1 large can mushroom soup
grated extra-sharp cheddar
   cheese

1½ pounds boiled and peeled
   new potatoes
salt and pepper

Fry bacon with onion until cooked. Strain off the fat. Stir in mushroom soup and heat. Slice potatoes in an earthenware dish. Season with salt and pepper. Pour mushroom soup mixture over potatoes and top with grated cheese. Brown in the oven. Six servings.

Pork and Potato Pie

1 pound potatoes, parboiled
   and peeled
1 pound veal or pork,
   cut finely
3 tablespoons butter
2 cups chicken stock
1 teaspoon crushed juniper
   berries or mixed herbs

⅔ cup cider
salt and pepper
potato (or short) pastry, using
   1½ times recipe on page 108
light cream

Fry veal for ten minutes, pork a bit longer to make sure it is cooked through. Place potatoes and meat in pie dish. Add stock and cider, herbs, salt and pepper to taste. Cover with pie crust and place pie funnel in center. Brush with light cream. Bake for one hour in 350 degree oven. Six servings.

Potato and Cream Cheese Sandwiches

1 pound mashed potatoes
1 large egg, separated
4 tablespoons butter
4 tablespoons grated cheese with
   a good strong flavor

salt and pepper
cream cheese

Beat the yolk thoroughly into potatoes. Add butter, grated cheese and seasoning. Whip the white until it stands in peaks and fold it into the potato mixture, with a feather touch. Place in mounds on a greased baking tray and cook until golden brown in a hot oven. Cool slightly and just before serving put them together like meringues with cream cheese. Four servings.

Adrien's Cheese Cake

Adrien is the chef of Chalet de Telebar Restaurant at Meribel aux Alps, the Swiss ski resort where Brigitte Bardot likes to hide away in the winter.

1 pound potatoes, grated	*salt and pepper*
½ pound grated cheese	*1 cup milk*
½ teaspoon Tabasco sauce	*parsley and chives*

Mix grated potatoes with cheese and seasoning. Add milk. Turn into buttered casserole and cook slowly until brown (about one hour). To serve, turn upside down and cover with finely chopped parsley mixed with chives. Four servings.

Girl-Talk Potatoes

My health-conscious girl friends who vow they "never eat potatoes" always fall for these when I make them.

4 large potatoes	*2 tablespoons butter*
2 hard-boiled eggs, chopped	*paprika to taste*
small cup of cottage or cream cheese	*finely chopped chives (optional)*
2 tablespoons strong grated cheese	*¼ cup sour cream*

Cook potatoes in boiling water for ten minutes until they are half cooked. Peel and cut in half. Carefully scrape out centers with a teaspoon so that halves do not break. Blend together the filling of eggs, chives, potato centers, butter, cheeses and paprika, and stuff each potato half, packing it fairly tightly. Put halves together again and lay them side by side in an ovenproof dish. Pour sour cream over each. Bake in a 350 degree oven for thirty minutes. Any left-over bacon can be chopped up and added or, for a more piquant taste, try one small anchovy fillet finely chopped for each potato. Serve with crisp cucumber or watercress salad. Eight servings.

Turkish Potato Balls

I am very fond of these because they are lighter than Anglophile potato rissoles. I persuade myself that they are less fattening, too. Serve with broiled chicken or fish.

1 pound potatoes
¼ pound cottage cheese
1 tablespoon chopped parsley
1 whole egg, chopped
salt and pepper

2 egg yolks, beaten with a little cold water
breadcrumbs
oil or fat for frying

Peel potatoes and boil until soft. Put them through a ricer to get them really smooth. Mix in the egg, cheese, seasoning and parsley. Mix well and break off into small pieces. Shape into balls and slightly flatten. Roll in egg yolk and then breadcrumbs. Fry in vegetable oil or fat. If you have plenty of parsley, fry some sprigs until crisp and sprinkle over the top just before serving. Four servings.

Brabanconne Potato Cocottes

This comes from the Belgium province of Brabanconne and makes a delicious supper dish also. Mix mashed potatoes with a bouquet of finely chopped fresh herbs. Thyme, mint, parsley, marjoram, basil and dill are all suitable. Add one third as much of finely grated parmesan or other strong cheese. Fill up cocotte dishes and sprinkle with fine breadcrumbs. Brown under broiler.

Yugoslavian Potato Cocottes

The Yugoslavs have their version of this lunchtime speciality.

2 pounds potatoes
¼ pound smoked bacon
6 tablespoons butter
½ pound cottage cheese

2 tablespoons home-made breadcrumbs
salt and pepper to taste

Boil potatoes in skins, peel and slice. Butter the inside of a deep-sided flame-proof dish and sprinkle with some of the breadcrumbs. Now place on them half the potatoes. Cut bacon into small pieces and fry until crisp. Sprinkle half on top of the potatoes. Meanwhile, melt cheese and butter over a low heat. Pour half the quantity over bacon and potatoes. Add another layer of potatoes and finish with a layer of bacon. Pour on rest of butter and cheese. Season to taste. Top with remaining breadcrumbs. Cook over moderate heat for twenty minutes without a lid. Place a strong plate over top of dish and turn upside down. Cut like a cake. Eight servings.

Rumanian Potato Cake

In the Rumanian version, hard-boiled eggs are added. I find it better to leave this one in the oven-proof dish in which it is cooked.

2 pounds potatoes
1 tablespoon butter
4-5 hard-boiled eggs, sliced
½ cup sour cream
salt and pepper

9 tablespoons strong-tasting grated cheese (a pungent cheddar is just as good as parmesan)

Boil potatoes in skins. Peel and slice. Butter an earthenware dish and place in it alternate layers of potatoes and eggs. Pour sour cream over. Salt and pepper to taste and cover with a blanket of cheese. Bake in a 350 degree oven for half an hour and crisp off, if necessary, under the broiler. Eight servings.

Vegetarian Potato Pie

This is a basic recipe which you can alter to suit the housekeeping purse.

1 pound potatoes
4 fresh tomatoes
handful of shallots
2 small leeks
4 tablespoons butter
1½ tablespoons flour
1 cup milk

4 ounces grated cheese
1 teaspoon French mustard
1 tablespoon pitted green olives, chopped
4 hard-boiled eggs, sliced
salt and pepper to taste

Parboil potatoes for fifteen minutes, peel and slice. Peel and slice tomatoes. Fry shallots and leeks in butter until golden. Make a sauce by melting butter and adding flour to form a roux. Blend in the milk. Add mustard and half the cheese. In a buttered casserole, place a layer of potatoes, cover with some of the leeks, then tomato slices, then sliced hard-boiled eggs. Make another layer, finishing with potatoes. Pour cheese sauce over all and finish with olives and rest of grated cheese. Dot with butter. Bake for thirty minutes until sizzling golden brown in a 350 degree oven. Finish under broiler if necessary. Four servings.

Potato Nests

Prepare duchesse potatoes as described on page 48, and using a forcing bag, pipe into the shape of birds' nests, on a cookie tin. Bake in a hot oven until firm and brown. Remove from oven and fill with any creamy sauce flavored with, for instance, chopped kidneys, sweetbreads, sweet corn, asparagus tips, tuna fish, chicken or mushrooms. Eight servings.

Irish Potato Ring

My Canadian sister-in-law, Sally, who now lives in New Zealand, gave me this recipe and swears it is Irish. I doubt it, but wherever it comes from it is a pleasant lunchtime experience.

1 pound package of frozen spinach	1 tablespoon onion juice
6 large potatoes	1 beaten egg
⅔ cup heavy cream	1½ teaspoons salt
1 stick plus 2 tablespoons soft butter	¼ teaspoon pepper
	½ teaspoon ground mace

Cook, drain and chop spinach. Boil potatoes, peel and put through a ricer. Add cream, butter, onion juice, egg and seasoning to potatoes. Pile in a well-buttered one-and-a-half quart ring or mold. Bake in moderate oven for twenty minutes. Unmold and fill center with any of the following: creamed chipped beef and eggs, creamed fish or chicken, creamed sweetbreads or buttered baby beets. Eight servings.

Pisto from Portugal

1 pound small new potatoes	1 pound zucchini
1 sliced onion	olive oil for frying

Parboil scrubbed potatoes, and slice. Fry onion until golden in olive oil (not butter). Add sliced potatoes and zucchini and fry gently. The zucchini should be slightly undercooked, with a bite. Four servings.

Pittsburgh Potatoes

Serve as a luncheon dish with a salad. It is also a good meat "stretcher" for the main course and goes well with chicken, roast meats, sausages or fried liver.

1 onion	1½ cups white sauce
1 pound potatoes	½ teaspoon salt
1 small jar pimientos	pinch of curry powder (optional)
¼ pound mild grated cheese	

Cook the potatoes and onion in their skins in boiling salted water for five minutes. Peel while still hot and cut potatoes into cubes. Mince onion. Place vegetables in a buttered baking dish and top with the pimiento cut into fine ribbons. Make a rich white sauce to which you have added at the last moment the curry powder and grated cheese. Pour over potatoes and cook in a 350 degree oven for twenty minutes. Brown under broiler. Four servings.

Potato Gnocchi from Italy

Every experienced cook knows that you can adapt many recipes and make them with potatoes. It may seem strange that something so Italian as gnocchi tastes good with potatoes instead of pasta.

Gnocchi:
  1 pound potatoes
  ¾ cup flour
  1 egg
salt and pepper
  1 teaspoon basil
parmesan cheese for topping

Sauce:
  1 slice streaky bacon
  1 large onion, chopped
  2 tablespoons flour
  1 large can peeled tomatoes, because the flavor is more pungent than fresh
  1 tablespoon butter or oil
  garlic to taste

Peel potatoes thinly and boil in salted water until tender. Meanwhile, make the sauce: Cut the bacon into small pieces and sauté in the butter with the onion. Add flour and cook for a few minutes without browning. Add tomatoes and season to taste. Then drain potatoes and mash well, adding the flour, egg, salt and pepper and basil. With your hands make a long roll about half an inch thick. Cut into inch lengths. Drop into a pan of boiling salted water and simmer gently for five minutes. Drain and put into serving dish. Pour hot tomato sauce over it and sprinkle with parmesan. Four servings.

American Potato Roll

This is really an inside-out shepherd's pie.

1 pound ground beef
1 onion
1 cup fresh breadcrumbs
salt and pepper and garlic to taste

a drop of tomato juice or milk to bind
2 well-beaten eggs
1 pound mashed potatoes

Mix together the beef, onion, breadcrumbs and seasoning. Add the eggs and bind with the tomato juice or milk. Spread the meat loaf out on a floured board, rolling like pastry into a rectangle shape. Fill the center with mashed potatoes right down the middle. Roll up like a parcel and place in buttered foil. Bake for one hour in a moderate oven, opening the foil for the last half hour to allow meat to brown. Just before serving, you can add a can of tomato soup to make a dazzling sauce. Four servings.

Curried Potatoes

6 medium potatoes
2 tablespoons butter
2 tablespoons flour
1 tablespoon curry powder
1 cup chicken stock

1 small onion, chopped
for seasoning, add apples,
    raisins, currants
1 tablespoon marmalade

Boil or steam potatoes until they are firm. Peel and slice them. Melt butter and add flour to make a roux. Add curry powder and stir in stock and the rest of the curry ingredients. Simmer gently for twenty minutes and pour over potatoes. Serve with fried bread, croutons or papadums. Six servings.

Potato and Walnut Lakhes

2¼ cups grated potatoes
½ cup halved walnuts
2 eggs, beaten
6 tablespoons flour

salt and pepper
butter for frying
sour cream

Allow potatoes to soak for half an hour. Drain and dry in cloth. Add beaten eggs, flour, seasoning and walnuts. Fry in butter like pancakes. Serve with sour cream. Four servings.

Swiss Rosti

This is the most popular dish in Switzerland. In Zurich it is served just as it is; in Berne fried onion is added. Press one pound boiled potatoes through a ricer. Fry in lard or oil until brown underneath. When the underneath is brown, turn upside down on a plate. Serve with cold meats. Four to six servings.

Fish Pie

This is the basis for a more extravagant pie, though mussels or shrimps can also be added.

1 pound mashed potatoes
1 pound cod or haddock
1 cup milk
salt and pepper to taste
1 bay leaf

4 tablespoons butter, divided
2 tablespoons flour
1 tablespoon curry powder
4 hard-boiled eggs, sliced
breadcrumbs

Simmer fish in milk, to which salt, pepper and bay leaf have been added, for ten minutes. Remove fish from liquid and while hot, skin and flake into pieces. Place in bottom of fireproof dish. Discard bay leaf and strain liquid. Make a roux with two tablespoons butter and flour and pour in liquid, adding a little more milk if required. Stir in curry powder. Lay eggs on bed of fish. Pour sauce over. Top with creamy mashed potatoes. Sprinkle with finely ground breadcrumbs and dot with rest of butter. Bake at 400 degrees until brown. Four servings.

Potato Soups

The simplest and most indulgent form of using potatoes is in soups. In basic recipes potatoes can act not only as a common denominator in creamy soups but as an emulsifier, blending a dozen different flavors into one harmonious whole.

One of the most outstanding soups that I have ever tasted is also one of the most inexpensive to make. The recipe was given to me by a friend who acquired it from an American clavichord player. It has a very special earthy taste. Your guests look puzzled and ask: "Is it artichoke or has it a chestnut base?" The bouquet is so subtle that it is difficult to discern. One thing for certain, if you wash the potatoes thoroughly, it is not a muddy taste, but a subtle, nutty, expensive taste.

Potato Skin Soup

The peelings from 2 pounds
   of potatoes
1 onion, chopped
parsley or chives to garnish

4 tablespoons butter
4 cups stock from chicken or
   beef bones, or even a cube
light cream if necessary

Wash potatoes lovingly and peel, not too thinly. Cook chopped onion and potato skins in butter until the onion and peel are tender. Add stock, bring to boil, remove and blend on high speed. Reheat, adding light cream if it is too thick, and serve sprinkled with chopped chives or parsley. On special occasions a teaspoon of chopped walnuts sprinkled on instead of the parsley is sheer heaven. Four servings.

In the late eighteenth century, England's Lancashire had a vast home industry in cotton weaving. The cotton worker's home was a miniature unhygienic factory, with the women and children picking the cotton and the men weaving it. Overnight all this changed, when Hargreaves invented his "spinning jenny" in 1767 and Crompton his "mule" in 1775; the whole industry of spinning took on a new dimension. Small mills sprang up all along the Pennine streams and then with more elaborate machinery and on a larger scale, in the plains below. The home weaver was finished forever. Hundreds of families now faced destitution.

Thomas Bayley Potter, the Liberal M.P. for the district, was gravely concerned for the health of the people. He asked the London chef Francatelli to compile a small book called *Cookery for the People*, which he then proceeded to distribute among the impoverished weavers.

I am indebted to my friends—his granddaughters, the Misses Katharine and Dorothy Potter of Ramsden in Oxfordshire—for lending me this book. It contains such doubtful delicacies as stewed sheep's head and barley broth, baked tripe and cow's head soup, and the potato soup must be the most modest on record. It is, however, nourishing and a palatable "filler."

Famine Soup

2 pounds potatoes
4 cups water
6 onions
salt and pepper to taste

4 tablespoons dripping or a small chunk of bacon cut up into pieces
parsley to garnish

Wash and slice potatoes, add the rest of the ingredients and place to simmer slowly for one hour, taking care to stir the stew frequently from the bottom to prevent it from burning. Add more water if necessary. If you have a blender, put the soup in it. Otherwise place through a sieve. Sprinkle with parsley before serving. Six servings.

Potato Soup

My own variation of this soup is richer and, therefore, even more nourishing. It is a great favorite with my god-children.

4 medium potatoes
1 quart milk
1 onion
3 tablespoons butter, divided
1 tablespoon flour
1 teaspoon curry powder

1½ teaspoons salt
⅛ teaspoon pepper
¼ teaspoon celery salt
parsley or toasted almonds
   to garnish

Cook potatoes in boiling salted water, and peel. Rub through a sieve or ricer. Scald milk with onion. Remove onion and add milk slowly to potatoes, mixing with a wire whisk. Melt half the butter, add flour, curry, pepper and salt and celery salt. Stir into hot soup. Boil one minute, then pour through a strainer. Add remaining butter and serve sprinkled with parsley or sliver of toasted almonds. Six servings.

Swiss Potato Soup

2 small turnips
6 medium potatoes
2 cups boiling water or stock
2 cups hot milk

2 tablespoons butter
1 tablespoon minced onion
2 tablespoons flour
pepper, salt and mace

Wash, peel and chop turnips and potatoes. Boil in water or stock until vegetables are soft, for about ten minutes. Put vegetables through a sieve or in a blender. Add milk and reheat. Melt butter in another saucepan, add onion and cook until golden. Stir in flour to make a roux. Stir in potato and turnip purée slowly. Season. Give it a few turns with a whisk and serve with croutons or grated cheese. Four servings.

Every country has its great soups. Vichyssoise was created early in the twentieth century by master chef Louis Diat of the Ritz Carlton Hotel in New York. It was a sophisticated version of the humble paysanne potato and leek soup of his boyhood in France. Today it is served on the menus of more great restaurants than any other soup. It is delicious hot but even more desirable on a warm summer's evening served chilled with finely chopped chives. It is better made the day before so that the flavors have time to infuse.

Vichyssoise

4 leeks	salt and pepper to taste
8 tablespoons butter	few grains nutmeg
4 cups chicken stock	1 cup heavy cream
1 stalk celery	chives to garnish
4 potatoes	

Cook finely chopped leeks in butter until tender. Add stock, celery, peeled and sliced potatoes and seasoning, and cook until potatoes and celery are tender. Place in the blender or through a sieve. Just before serving, stir in cream and sprinkle with chives. Four servings.

Potato and Cheese Soup

1 small onion	1 quart water
1 carrot	4 tablespoons grated cheddar
2 tablespoons butter	or parmesan cheese
2 pounds potatoes	1 cup milk
salt and pepper to taste	

Cut up vegetables in small pieces. Melt the butter and saute the onion and carrot for a couple of minutes but do not let them color. Add the potatoes and seasoning and the water. Simmer with lid on the saucepan for fifteen minutes. Put through a sieve or in a blender. Add milk and reheat. Sprinkle the grated cheese before serving.

Potato Dumplings

In Rumania tiny potato dumplings are served with strong clear soup. Since any good consommé is time-consuming, these help to give that homemade touch to the canned variety.

3 medium potatoes	salt and pepper and grated
1 tablespoon flour	nutmeg to taste
1 tablespoon light cream	4 cups consommé
1 egg	parsley or chives to garnish

Boil, peel and mash potatoes. Add the flour, cream, egg and seasonings. Shape into tiny dumplings, each as big as a large grape. Simmer in 4 cups of clear consommé. Serve with chopped parsley or chives.

Potato and Smoked Haddock Soup

½ pound potatoes, peeled and
   sliced
4 shallots or 1 leek, using
   only the white
2 tablespoons butter

1 small smoked haddock
2 cups chicken stock
pepper and salt to taste
½ cup heavy cream
parsley to garnish

Prepare vegetables and fry in butter for five minutes. Steep haddock in a pan of boiling water for five minutes (this takes out some of the coloring and makes the fish easy to separate from the skin and bone). Add stock, pepper and salt to vegetables and simmer for thirty minutes. Sieve or place in blender. Add flaked fish and cook very gently for ten minutes longer. Pour boiling hot into soup cups and pour the cold cream into a well in the center. Sprinkle with parsley. Four servings.

Mulligatawny Soup

From the Eastern provinces of India, this soup has a delightful fruity, spicy flavor.

½ pound peeled and sliced
   potatoes
1 small onion
1 medium carrot
1 cooking apple

4 tablespoons butter
1 tablespoon curry powder
2 teaspoons tomato purée
2 cups beef stock
salt and pepper
rind and juice of 1 lemon

Peel and slice vegetables and apple. Melt butter in soup pot and fry them all with the curry and tomato purée for five minutes to sweat the flavor out. Add stock, salt and pepper, and simmer with the lid on for forty-five minutes. Sieve or blend and add lemon juice. Garnish with slivers of the rind of the lemon. Four servings.

Potato and Watercress Soup

½ pound potatoes
1 medium onion
2 cups chicken stock

1 bunch watercress
2 tablespoons butter
½ cup milk or cream

Peel and slice potatoes and onion. Saute in butter until golden. Cover with stock and cook for fifteen minutes. Wash watercress, select four of the best sprigs for garnishing, and set these aside. Add the rest, including stalks, to soup. Simmer a further fifteen minutes. Put in a blender or through a sieve. Add milk or cream for an even richer flavor. Float a sprig of watercress on the surface of each bowl of soup before serving. Four servings.

Whenever I am in New York I rush to the Grand Central Railway Station to have clam and potato chowder. Originating in Britanny— "faire la chaudiere" literally translated means "supply the kettle"—the chowder became a favorite in New England and Newfoundland cooking. A chowder is a fish meal in itself. I make my chowder with mussels which, while lacking the delicacy of clams, have an attractive pungent taste.

Mussel Chowder

½ pound any white fish
1 tablespoon butter
1 onion, peeled and sliced
1 carrot, peeled and sliced
2 cups cold water

½ bay leaf and
1 sprig thyme, in cheesecloth bag
1 cup diced parboiled potatoes
1 cup shelled mussels
parsley to garnish

Remove skin and bones from fish. Melt butter in a deep saucepan. Sauté onions and carrot until they have softened. Add fish, water, bay leaf and thyme. Simmer for one hour. Remove herbs and add potatoes. Cook until they are soft. Add freshly cooked and chopped mussels or mussels bought in a jar of brine, not vinegar. Bring to boil for three minutes and serve sprinkled with parsley. Four servings.

Crécy Soup

½ pound potatoes, peeled and sliced
½ pound carrots, peeled and sliced
1 medium onion, chopped
2 stalks celery, chopped

1 clove crushed garlic
4 tablespoons butter
2 cups chicken stock
½ cup milk
salt and pepper
finely grated carrot to garnish

Fry prepared vegetables in butter and garlic for five minutes until all the butter is absorbed. Add stock and simmer for one hour. Before serving, sieve or blend. Add milk, salt and pepper to taste, and sprinkle with grated carrot before serving. Four servings.

Potato Suppers

As the main meal of the day, call it what you will—dinner or supper—the potato is invaluable. It has nourishment, substance, character; and treated with loving reverence it can even be flamboyant.

Portuguese Potatoes with Cheese Sauce

6 medium potatoes, peeled

3 tablespoons olive oil

1 medium onion, finely chopped

1 can (1 pound 12 ounces) whole tomatoes, drained

2 green chili peppers, seeded and chopped

1 can (8 ounces) tomato sauce

1 teaspoon chili powder

4 to 6 slices Monterey Jack or mozzarella cheese

4 hard-cooked eggs, sliced

8 slices bacon, cooked and drained

Boil potatoes until tender. While potatoes are cooking, heat oil in a heavy skillet and cook onion until soft and translucent. Add tomatoes, chili peppers, tomato sauce and chili powder. Simmer for 10 minutes. Arrange slices of cheese on top of sauce and continue to simmer until cheese is soft and melting. Arrange potatoes on platter and garnish with sliced eggs and bacon. Serve with sauce. Six servings.

Shepherd's Pie

This is still one of my favorite foods. You can use minced cold meat but for a really juicy pie use uncooked meat.

1 pound potatoes

1 pound lean ground beef

2 peeled chopped onions

1 cup beef broth

¼ pound sliced mushrooms (optional)

½ cup hot milk

4 tablespoons butter, divided

4 tablespoons flour

Melt 2 tablespoons butter in saucepan, add onion, fry until golden. Add meat and turn until the juices are sealed in. Stir in stock. Season to taste. Cook for another ten minutes. Stir in flour to thicken and add sliced mushrooms. Place in buttered pie dish. Stir remaining butter and milk into mashed potatoes and beat well. Spread evenly over meat. Rake with a fork towards the center. Bake in 350 degree oven for twenty minutes. Put under broiler to brown before serving or turn up the oven to high temperature. Four servings.

Lancashire Hot Pot

1 pound potatoes	1 cup chicken stock
1½ pounds middle neck of lamb	salt and pepper
2 large onions, sliced	butter

Trim meat and cut into small pieces. Peel potatoes and cut into slices. Take an ovenproof dish and add first a layer of meat, then sliced onions, then potatoes, another layer of meat and a further one of onions, adding salt and pepper to taste, for each layer. Finish with a good layer of potatoes. Pour stock over and cover with a lid. Bake for three hours very slowly, adding small dabs of butter if potatoes look too dry, or more stock. Brown potatoes at the end under broiler. Four servings.

Potato Meat Loaf

1 pound potatoes	garlic or bay leaf to taste
1 pound raw minced beef	salt and pepper
parsley, chopped	1 egg
1 large onion, finely chopped	soy sauce to garnish
1 tablespoon Worcestershire sauce	

Peel potatoes and grate. It does not matter if they discolor. Mix with beef, parsley, onion, Worcestershire sauce, seasoning, garlic. Bind with the egg. Place bay leaf in bottom of a two pound loaf pan. Fill with mixture. Cover liberally with soy sauce in criss-cross pattern. Bake in 350 degree oven for one hour. Turn out and serve, if possible, soy side up. Four servings.

Potato Roly-Poly

1 pound potatoes, boiled, peeled and mashed	4 hard-boiled eggs
1 pound sausage meat	1 egg, beaten
1 onion	3 tablespoons white breadcrumbs
½ teaspoon thyme	3 tablespoons bacon fat
1 tablespoon chopped parsley	1 can tomato soup

Blend mashed potatoes and sausage meat with herbs. Shape into a roll and make a hollow down the center. Place a hard-boiled egg at regular intervals. Roll to close. Brush with beaten egg and roll in bread crumbs. Bake in 350 degree oven with bacon fat and cook for one hour. In the last quarter of an hour, pour a can of tomato soup over it. Four servings.

Shropshire Fidget Pie

1 pound potatoes
½ pound apples
½ pound streaky bacon, cut
   in small pieces
1 tablespoon brown sugar

salt and pepper
½ cup stock or ale
potato pastry, according to
   directions on page 108

Peel and cut potatoes and apples in slices. Mix with bacon and place in a greased pie dish. Sprinkle with sugar and seasoning. Cover with stock or ale. Roll out pastry and cover the filling. Insert pie funnel. Glaze with milk. Bake for one and a quarter to one and a half hours in a 350 degree oven. Four to six servings.

Pepper Hot Pot

1 pound neck of lamb
2 lamb's kidneys
2 peeled onions
1 large green pepper

salt and pepper to taste
1½ cups stock
1½ pounds new potatoes
1 teaspoon paprika

Cut the meat into small sections and the skinned and cored kidneys into quarters. Place with the sliced onions in a casserole. Add pepper and salt, and the green pepper cut into matchstick strips. Pour stock on and cook for half an hour in a covered pot in a slow oven. Lift off lid and pop in scrubbed potatoes neatly arranged on top. Cook another quarter of an hour, then lift off lid for last quarter of an hour. Sprinkle with paprika before serving. Four servings.

Plukfisk

Plukfisk sounds better than the English translation, "Stewed Cod." It has been a family standby in Danish homes for generations. There, it is made from the left-overs of boiled cod, relating the recipe to the amount you have. But the basic recipe is easy to follow and I think a delicious family supper.

2 tablespoons butter
1 tablespoon flour
1 cup light cream
1 teaspoon French mustard
salt and pepper
1 pound boiled cod, boned
   and flaked

1 pound cold boiled potatoes,
   sliced
additional cold butter for each
   serving
parsley, chopped

Make a white sauce from the butter, flour and cream. Add salt, pepper and mustard. Stir in sliced potatoes and flaked fish. Place a lump of cold butter in the center of each plate when serving, with a sprinkling of parsley. Four servings.

King Size Sausage Rolls

Prepare one and a half times the potato short pastry on page 108, roll to about an eighth-inch thickness and divide into four. Skin 1 pound sausages and divide into four. Fill each roll with the sausage meat and brush edges of pastry with milk before folding over. Make three cuts diagonally across the top. Bake for twenty minutes in a 350 degree oven and serve with a rich tomato sauce or brown gravy. Four servings.

Danish Biksemad

Much better than serving up left-overs from a cold joint when the meat looks weary, is to make a good old-fashioned Danish "Biksemad"—fried meat and potatoes.

1 pound left-over meat	Worcestershire sauce
2 onions, chopped	salt and pepper to taste
4 tablespoons butter	4 eggs
2 pounds boiled potatoes, diced	

Cut meat into small dice. Brown onions in butter and then add cold meat. Turn until it is warmed through and finally add diced potatoes with salt, pepper and a drop of Worcestershire sauce. When everything has amalgamated, serve piping hot with a fried egg on top. Four servings.

Italian Potato Pie

2 tablespoons olive oil	3 tablespoons butter, melted
4 Italian sausages	parmesan cheese
2 cups diced cooked chicken	1 package frozen chopped spinach, cooked according to package directions
1 teaspoon seasoned salt	
½ teaspoon nutmeg	
1¾ cups white sauce, divided	6 or 8 sliced mushrooms
2 large potatoes, peeled and sliced about ⅛" thick	2½ tablespoons olive oil
	salt and pepper

Heat oil in a heavy skillet. Remove sausage skins and brown the sausages in olive oil. Add chicken, salt and nutmeg. Drain off any excess oil and add 1 cup of white sauce. Heap this mixture onto the center of an oven-proof serving plate. Arrange potato slices around and on top of the meat mixture, brush them with 3 tablespoons melted butter and sprinkle generously with the parmesan cheese. Bake for 35 to 40 minutes in a preheated 450 degree oven or until potatoes are browned and tender. Drain the spinach well, chop it, and add ¾ cup white sauce. Mix thoroughly. Salt and pepper to taste. Sauté mushrooms in 2½ tablespoons oil. When pie is removed from oven, place the spinach on top and finally the mushrooms. Four servings.

Good Sauces
and Stuffings

During the winter months, when potatoes lose some of their appeal and become floury, it is as well to dress them up. Here are some sauces that rejuvenate canned new potatoes, boiled potatoes or potatoes baked in their jackets.

Sour Cream Dressing

½ cup sour cream
2 hard-boiled egg yolks
¼ teaspoon sugar
1 tablespoon wine vinegar
½ teaspoon salt

Mash egg yolks in bowl with sugar and salt. Gradually thin with vinegar and finally add sour cream.

Crème Chantilly

1 tablespoon mashed potatoes
1 teaspoon mustard
½ cup heavy cream
1 tablespoon wine or cider vinegar
salt and pepper to taste

Whip cream stiffly and add other ingredients slowly.

Barbecue Sauce

This is delicious with steamed fish or boiled chicken if a few capers are added.

1 teaspoon salt
1 teaspoon chili powder
1 teaspoon celery or dill seed
¼ cup brown sugar
¼ cup wine or cider vinegar
¼ cup tomato sauce
2 cups water
few drops of Tabasco sauce

Mix all together and bring to boiling point. It is better left for twenty-four hours before using so that the flavors all merge with each other. Serve hot or cold.

Horseradish Sauce

½ cup heavy cream or evaporated milk
3 tablespoons mayonnaise
2 tablespoons freshly grated horseradish
1 teaspoon mustard
½ teaspoon salt
few grains of cayenne

Beat cream until stiff and fold in the other ingredients. Superb with potatoes baked in their jackets.

Piquant Sauce

2 tablespoons chopped onion
4 tablespoons green pepper
2 tablespoons butter
2 fresh tomatoes or half a
   cup of canned tomatoes

¼ cup sliced mushrooms
1⅓ cups brown sauce or gravy
8 olives, pitted
salt and pepper
sherry or Madeira to taste

Cook onion and pepper with butter for five minutes. Add tomatoes, mushrooms and olives, and cook for about two minutes. Add brown sauce, salt and pepper and sherry or Madeira.

Cheese Sauce

2 tablespoons butter
2 tablespoons flour
1 cup scalded milk

¼ teaspoon salt
few grains of pepper
½ teaspoon curry powder
¾ cup grated cheese

Melt butter in small saucepan and stir in flour to make a roux. Pour on scalded milk, gradually whisking with a wire beater so that no lumps form. Add salt and pepper to taste, blend in the curry powder, and lastly stir in the cheese.

Béchamel Sauce

Béchamel sauce, which was created and dedicated to the Marquis of Béchamel in the reign of Louis XIV, is the simple white sauce known in every kitchen and made from a roux of butter and flour. Add to this hot milk which has previously been boiled with an onion stuck with a clove and peppercorn. This is an excellent base for many potato sauces.

Sorrel Béchamel

This gives a surprisingly piquant taste to new potatoes.

1 pound sorrel (sour grass)
½ cup boiling water
1 tablespoon sugar

salt and pepper to taste
1 pint béchamel sauce

Blanch sorrel in hot water until it becomes limp. Add rest of ingredients and whizz in a blender or put through a sieve.

Velouté Sauce

Velouté sauce is made in a similar way to béchamel, with chicken or veal stock replacing the milk.

Mushroom Sauce

1 pint velouté sauce
½ pound mushrooms

2 tablespoons butter
dash lemon juice

Slice the mushrooms and cook very slowly in butter until they literally sweat but do not brown. Add to velouté sauce and put all in a blender or pass through a sieve. Stir in lemon juice.

Mushroom Potato Sauce

¼ pound mushrooms
2 tablespoons butter
1 cup chicken stock

1 tablespoon mashed potatoes
salt and pepper

Scrub mushrooms but do not peel. Slice and cook for five minutes in half the butter. Add stock and simmer five minutes longer. Put through the blender or a sieve. Make a roux of the remaining butter and the potatoes. Add the liquified mushrooms. Season with salt and pepper.

Mornay Sauce

2 cups béchamel sauce
1 teaspoon Worcestershire
   sauce

¼ pound grated Swiss or
   parmesan cheese, or a
   combination of both

The brown sauce that has become the leitmotif of all bourgeois cooking throughout Europe need not be the ghastly thick mockery that appears on our tables. Its consistency should be velvety and the taste indefinable. When the béchamel sauce has thickened, stir in the grated cheese and Worcestershire sauce.

Mousselaine Sauce

2 cups velouté sauce
2 egg yolks

salt and pepper to taste
1 tablespoon lemon juice

Whip all together until a pale yellow creamy mixture results.

Roosevelt Sauce

A favorite of that great American gourmet, Theodore Roosevelt. Many a deal has been clinched over this sauce. Looks and tastes pretty with small new potatoes.

1 pound tomatoes (preferably fresh) which have been skinned by dousing them in boiling water or holding over a flame
2 tablespoons butter

1 teaspoon paprika
salt and pepper to taste
tomato purée
1 tablespoon cornstarch

Sauté tomatoes gently in the butter, add paprika and seasoning. Measure tomatoes in a cup and add equal quantity of slightly sweetened tomato purée. Heat, and thicken with cornstarch if necessary.

Oriental Sauce

The days of using port, brandy and sherry ad lib in the kitchen for everyday cooking are over, and so sometimes we must substitute with amusing flavors from the normal kitchen cupboard.

1 pint ordinary brown gravy
1 tablespoon dark marmalade

Whisk and serve piping hot. Adds a tang to boiled potatoes.

Espagnole Sauce

2 tablespoons butter
4 slices streaky bacon
1 small onion
1 carrot

1 teaspoonful dried herbs
1 bay leaf
4 tablespoons flour
2 cups beef stock

Cut bacon into small pieces and fry until crisp. Add butter, minced onion and thinly sliced carrot. Cook until vegetables are soft. Add bay leaf and mixed herbs, and sprinkle flour over, mixing vigorously into a roux. Work in the beef stock and if there are a few lumps, do not bother about them. Leave to cook slowly for half an hour. If you like a deeper color, add commercial gravy coloring. Strain before serving.

Hollandaise Sauce

When young chefs were interviewed for a position in France at the turn of the century, when cooking was at its most spectacular and extravagant, they were asked to boil six eggs and make Hollandaise sauce. The rich eggy flavor of the sauce gives added dimension to new potatoes. I often serve this topped with freshly chopped dill as a first course during the summer.

about 1 tablespoon lemon juice
salt and pepper to taste
1 tablespoon cold water

½ cup butter, divided
4 egg yolks

Heat gently, in a double boiler, lemon juice, water, salt and pepper. Divide butter into four pieces. Add egg yolks and quarter of the butter, stirring rapidly in one direction. When the butter has been absorbed, add another quarter. Repeat until all the butter has been used. Remove from heat and continue to beat for two or three minutes longer until a thick sauce looking like mayonnaise appears. Add more drops of lemon juice if you like a tart flavor. If at any time due to the room temperature being too warm the mixture should curdle, beat in one or two tablespoons of cold water to rebind.

Curry Sauce

1 small onion, sliced
2 tablespoons butter
2 tablespoons flour

1 teaspoon curry powder
2 cups chicken stock
salt and pepper to taste
sweet chutney (optional)

Sauté onion in butter until soft and pale yellow. Stir in flour mixed with curry powder. Add stock slowly and cook over gentle heat for ten minutes. Season with salt and pepper. For additional flavor add one tablespoon of sweet chutney.

Hot Mayonnaise

This is an excellent way of dressing up new potatoes during the winter months.

2 egg yolks
2 tablespoons olive oil
1 tablespoon vinegar
¼ cup hot water

salt and pepper
1 tablespoon finely chopped gherkins

Add oil slowly to egg yolks. Pour on vinegar and water gradually. Stir and cook over hot water until thickened. Season and add gherkins.

Peppered Potatoes

In Denmark the Christmas goose is usually stuffed with prunes and apples. In our home we prefer to do this for one end of the bird and in the other we have peppered potatoes.

1 pound potatoes, parboiled and peeled
1 onion

coarse salt, milled black pepper
3 tablespoons butter

Dice potatoes into half-inch squares, chop onions very finely, add pepper and salt. Place half the stuffing in the bird and then add butter. Continue with the rest of the stuffing.

Herb Stuffing

This is a fine, robust stuffing for chicken or any meat. When using for breast of lamb or veal, two diced slices of streaky bacon give added flavor.

1 pound hot mashed potatoes
3 tablespoons butter
½ teaspoon salt
¼ teaspoon pepper
grated rind of 1 lemon

¼ teaspoon mixed herbs
1 teaspoon parsley
1 teaspoon chopped onion
1 beaten egg

Mix potato and butter in a bowl. Add salt, pepper, lemon rind, herbs, parsley and onion. Beat in the egg and the stuffing is ready. Fresh herbs make all the difference to this stuffing. Chopped raw celery is also a good addition.

Potato Picnics

Sandwiches should be forbidden at picnics. Made in the proper way the sandwich is a superb work of art, but it should be eaten within a stone's throw of the kitchen, when the egg is still warm and buttery, the tomato chaste and firm, and the cucumber glistening with juice. There are so many other foods that transport better, and here the potato comes into its own. Potato Scotch Eggs, Sausage Snowballs and Potato Cheese Footballs are not only filling but amusing for either school lunches or picnics.

Potato Scotch Eggs

4 hard-boiled eggs
1¼ pounds duchesse potato mixture (page 48)

1 egg
breadcrumbs

Divide potato mixture into four parts and pack tightly round each hard-boiled egg. Coat with beaten egg and roll in breadcrumbs. (Homemade ones are not only cheaper but taste much better than those stale, dried-out commercial ones). Deep fry in smoking fat, if possible, or fry in a shallow pan and keep turning the eggs over and over until golden brown. It only takes a few minutes. Drain on kitchen paper and serve with homemade tomato sauce or tomato ketchup. Four servings.

Sausage Snowballs with Tomato Sauce

Use four boiled sausages, or sausage meat that has first been poached in water, instead of the eggs, and proceed as above. These are delicious served with a strong sauce made from fresh tomatoes that have been skinned, lots of garlic, pepper and salt, and a pinch of sugar. Whip in the blender until it is frothy and light. A drop of Tabasco or Worcestershire sauce gives an added tang. This sauce is not cooked but served just as it is. Four servings.

Potato Cheese Footballs

These can be wrapped in foil to keep them warm.

1¼ pounds potatoes
4 tablespoons butter
4 ounces grated extra-sharp cheddar cheese
salt and pepper

4 hard-boiled eggs
1 tablespoon chopped chives or parsley
1 beaten egg
breadcrumbs

Cook potatoes until soft, peel and mash with butter, cheese, salt and pepper. Chop the hard-boiled eggs coarsely and mix into the potato, together with the chopped chives. Divide the mixture into eight parts and roll into small balls. Roll in beaten egg and coat with breadcrumbs. Deep fry until golden brown and serve with a crisp green salad. The distinctive taste of watercress goes well with this light luncheon dish. Four servings.

I remember my first visit to the Derby not because of that enchanting tree-top ride on the top of a double decker bus that my American hostess had hired, nor that first glimpse of the Downs teeming with life, nor that grotty gypsy who misguidedly told me that I would marry a millionaire, but the picnic lunch. It consisted of warm chicken pasties, served with individual punnets of apple, cucumber and walnut salad in mayonnaise and finally a huge bowl of fresh strawberries with the stalks left on that one merely dunked into confectioners' sugar. I was also flabbergasted at the enormous thermos flask that each American husband carried. These, in fact, turned out to be filled with dry martinis and not coffee!

Chicken Pasties

potato short pastry, made as directed on page 108
¾ *pound peeled and diced potatoes*
½ *pound minced raw chicken meat*
pinch of paprika (optional)
¼ *pound mushrooms, chopped*
1 *cup thick white sauce to bind*
salt and pepper to taste
squeeze of lemon juice
milk

Roll out pastry and cut into four squares. Mix minced chicken, chopped mushrooms and diced potatoes, white sauce, pinch of paprika (optional), lemon juice, salt and pepper. Brush the edges of each square with milk, fill with chicken mixture and fold over into triangles. Brush each top with milk and make three slits to allow the steam to escape. Bake in 425 degree oven for ten minutes then turn down to 350 degrees and bake a further forty minutes until the top of the pastry has turned a golden brown. Four servings.

Cornish Pasties

The true Cornish pastry is another underrated picnic food. Do not make the mistake of using cooked meat for pasties. It is far better to turn that into Shepherd's Pie, for the pastry relies on juicy meat for its flavor and texture. I have tried many recipes but find that Mrs. Beeton's original is by far the best in its simplicity. She suggests beef but it can also be made from minced lean breast of lamb.

¼ *pound raw minced beef or lamb*
¼ *pound peeled and diced potatoes*
½ *teaspoon finely chopped onion*

mixed herbs to taste (parsley or lemon thyme add a subtle flavor but I have used dill seed with lamb)
2 tablespoons gravy or stock
potato short pastry, made as directed on page 108

Mince the meat finely. Dice potatoes, and add with the rest of the ingredients to the meat, giving it all a good stir. Divide the pastry into four equal rectangles. Pile the mixture into the center of each piece of pastry, wet the edges and pinch them together to make a welded seam. Prick pasties with a fork to allow the steam to escape. Bake in a hot oven for ten minutes, then reduce heat to moderate and cook for fifty minutes longer. Four servings.

Peanut Balls

Whether you serve them together in pies, casseroles or souffles, potato and sausage meat are a natural match. The bland kindness of the potatoes blends with the spicy saltiness and texture of the sausage. Try these as picnic teasers.

1 *cup mashed potatoes*
½ *pound pork sausage meat*
½ *teaspoon fresh mixed herbs (fresh herbs really are better here)*
1 *egg, beaten*
no salt but freshly ground pepper

½ *teaspoon freshly grated lemon peel*
½ *cup salted peanuts, chopped up until fine*
oil for frying

Mix together potatoes, sausage meat, herbs and lemon peel with half the beaten egg and a little milk if necessary. The mixture must be firm enough to roll into balls. Dip in remainder of egg and coat with peanuts. Fry in shallow pan, turning carefully until each side is cooked.

Potato Salads

POTATO SALADS

Potatoes for salads should be small and waxy. In Scandinavia where the housewife can choose from many different varieties of potatoes to suit her special dish, they are plainly labeled "salad potatoes." They are a little more expensive than ordinary ones but are much better. I have actually seen a Danish housewife hand-pick each salad potato, and the shopkeeper did not mind!

Jellied Potato Salad

1 pound diced boiled new
   potatoes
3 chopped spring onions
2 teaspoons chopped parsley
1 teaspoon chopped basil
2 teaspoons salt
2 green peppers

½ cup green peas
½ cup diced cucumber
¾ cup mayonnaise
¼ cup wine or cider vinegar
2 quarts aspic, prepared to the
   point of setting

Mix vegetables, mayonnaise, salt, and vinegar thoroughly but gently. Pour aspic to a depth of one inch in serving dish. Chill in refrigerator When the jelly is set, add salad in one layer. Pour rest of the aspic over and leave to set. Eight servings.

Sunflower Salad

4 large oranges
1 romaine lettuce
1 bunch watercress
2 cups diced new potatoes

¼ cup mayonnaise
¼ cup toasted almonds
few sprigs of mint

Peel oranges and separate into sections. Mix flesh with potatoes, mayonnaise and almonds. Line a bowl with romaine lettuce leaves standing up. Place salad in the center Sprinkle with chopped mint. Four servings.

German Potato Salad

1 large onion, chopped
1 pound cooked new potatoes
1 tablespoon vinegar

2 tablespoons butter
4 tablespoons mayonnaise
salt, pepper and sugar to taste

Sauté the finely chopped onion until golden. Add potatoes, vinegar, salt and pepper. Keep shaking the pan and finally stir in mayonnaise. Many people like a little sugar added to the vinegar to counteract the sharp vinegary taste. Serve with hot sausages. Four servings.

Sunshine Salad

1 pound tiny cooked new potatoes	1 tablespoon wine vinegar
½ cup sour cream	½ teaspoon salt
¼ teaspoon sugar	1 teaspoon French mustard
	2 hard-boiled eggs

Blend sour cream, sugar, vinegar, salt and mustard. Fold in new potatoes and turn into serving dish. Garnish with eggs cut into quarters and placed in a circle on top. Chill for half an hour. Four servings.

Potato and Tomato Salad

1 pound new potatoes	2½ tablespoons olive oil
5 skinned tomatoes	salt and pepper to taste
½ teaspoon French mustard	1½ tablespoons vinegar
1 teaspoon sugar	1 teaspoon chopped parsley

Slice potatoes and tomatoes. Place in layers alternately in serving bowl. Mix all the other ingredients and pour over. Top with parsley and chill. Four servings.

Winter Salad

I use two small cans of new potatoes rather than one large one simply because the potatoes are smaller and the salad looks more charming.

2 cans new potatoes	1 teaspoon mustard
1 apple	1 cup mayonnaise
1 cup chopped celery	salt and pepper
1 chopped parboiled onion	½ cup walnuts (optional)

Choose an apple with a red skin and cut into small dices unpeeled. Mix all ingredients in a bowl and chill. Four servings.

Sweet and Sour Salad

1 pound potatoes	⅔ cup plain yogurt
½ finely chopped raw onion	1 tablespoon raw or Demerara sugar
¼ pound cooked broad beans	
1 chopped gherkin (4oz.)	2 teaspoons French mustard
crystallized ginger, if you have any	salt to taste
	chopped parsley

Boil potatoes for ten minutes so that they remain firm, and peel. Drain well and cut into small dice. Mix with onion, beans, gherkin, ginger. Add the mustard, sugar and salt to yogurt and mix well. Pour over vegetables, mix with a spoon and cover with chopped parsley. Four servings.

Potato and Cheese Salad

6 small potatoes (new are
  better)
1 teaspoon finely chopped chives
¼ green pepper
1 teaspoon chopped parsley

½ cup French dressing
1 Boston lettuce
sliced tomatoes and cucumber
½ cup hard cheese, such as
  cheddar

Boil potatoes and peel and cube when cold. Mix chives, green pepper and parsley with French dressing. Add potatoes and stir thoroughly. Place into a mold, gently pressing down. Chill. For serving, turn mold on to a base of lettuce leaves and decorate with layers of sliced tomatoes, cucumber and grated cheese. Four servings.

Picnic Salad

4 medium-sized potatoes, boiled
  in their jackets
2 hard-boiled eggs
1 cup celery
½ cup chopped onion
1 red apple
¼ teaspoon celery seed

½ teaspoon salt
pepper to taste
mayonnaise to bind
1 tablespoon vinegar
mustard
capers (optional)

Peel and dice cold potatoes, add roughly chopped eggs, celery, onion, cut-up apple with skin left on, and seasonings. Dilute mayonnaise with vinegar and mustard to taste. Pour over potatoes and mix well. Sprinkle with capers. It carries well in a plastic container. Four servings.

Potato Salad Zenobia

6 medium potatoes, boiled in
  their jackets
2 medium Bermuda onions,
  sliced thin
¼ pound fresh mushrooms,
  sliced

1 cup salad olives with
  pimientos, chopped
2 tablespoons olive oil and
  2 tablespoons wine vinegar
  each, per layer of potato
freshly ground pepper and sea
  salt to taste

Peel potatoes and cut into cubes. Spread a layer in the bottom of the dish and add a layer each of the onions, sliced mushrooms and the salad olives. Sprinkle with olive oil and wine vinegar. Add pepper and salt to taste. Continue layering until all ingredients are used. Toss well, and refrigerate for several hours. The secret is to prepare while potatoes are still warm, and to use strong onions and a top quality olive oil.

There is no limit to the personal touches you can add—dill, basil, chopped green peppers, celery, dried, crushed red peppers, chopped hard-boiled egg, a hint of garlic in the olive oil, and so on. Eight or more servings.

Children's Choice

It has been estimated that if all the world's potato recipes were listed together and put into one volume, there would be enough to provide a different dish for every day for four years—1460 recipes.

Most children, however, are brought up on a potato horizon bounded in four ways—boiled, fried, chips and, if they are lucky, baked in their jackets. It is a tribute to the potato that it stands the test. Potatoes are a natural acceptable food for children, and in the Western world rank with bread, although they are much cheaper per pound. They have none of the sharpness of turnips, the yallory smell of cabbage or the opaque sliminess of onions. They do not have to be "sold" to children, who accept them with the same enjoyment as cornflakes and crispy toast.

Children consume an enormous amount of energy each day, whether it is during their hours at home or absorbing learning in the classroom. The presures on them from modern society are manifold, compared with life fifty years ago. This is why the potato is such a valuable ally to school children, providing each day a certain amount of carbohydrates which produce energy. Besides the carbohydrates, the potato also supplies protein, calcium, iron, vitamin C, and several of the B vitamins which are not present in such quantities in other carbohydrate foods.

Children need a large amount of nutrients, but because of their small stomachs, it is important that their meals not be too bulky. For their size, children therefore have a greater need for energy than adults. Children with big appetites, unless they are prone to a gland disturbance and therefore need medical attention, almost always reflect a real nutritional need and not greediness. If your child is constantly hungry, it is time to take stock of how you feed him or her.

I have chosen the following recipes specially for children because of their nutritional value. As children's stomachs have not yet learned that tiresome habit of dictating set food for breakfast, luncheon and dinner, these can be served any time of the day. Servings, as you will readily understand, are only approximate, since they are governed by age, size and unpredictable appetite!

Corn Pancakes

2 pounds raw potatoes	4 tablespoons milk
½ cup flour	1 pound can of whole
4 eggs	sweet corn

Grate raw potatoes and squeeze off surplus juice in a clean dish towel. Mix with the rest of the ingredients. Fry tablespoonfuls until golden brown. If a thinner pancake is required, pat the mixture flat when you put it in the pan. Four servings.

Potato Piglet

4 large potatoes for baking
4 sausages
4 ounces firm cheese, grated
2 tablespoons milk
2 tablespoons butter
salt and pepper

Scrub potatoes and prick all over with a fork. Bake in a moderate oven for one to one-and-a-half hours until soft. Cook sausages in the oven for last three quarters of an hour. When potatoes are done, cut lengthwise and scoop out center. Fluff up in a bowl with the milk, butter, salt and pepper, and grated cheese. Spoon back mixture into skins and lay a sausage along the center. Four servings.

Many children dislike the silky softness of a French omelette and prefer the bulkiness of a Spanish one which, in any case, is a meal in itself.

Spanish Omelette

1 pound boiled, peeled, sliced potatoes
4 tablespoons butter
½ pound sliced onions
¼ pound sliced tomatoes or green peppers
4 eggs
4 tablespoons cream
salt and pepper
4 ounces hard cheese, grated

If using green peppers, chop into small pieces and blanch in boiling water for five minutes. Melt butter in pan and add sliced onions. Cook slowly until golden brown. Add sliced potatoes, peppers or tomatoes. Beat eggs, cream, salt and pepper and pour over the vegetables, stirring gently once or twice. When the underside is firm and the omelette has nearly set, sprinkle grated cheese over it and brown under the broiler. Four servings.

Baked Bean Pie

½ pound cold left-over meat (chicken, lamb, beef or pork)
⅓ cup onions, minced
1 small can tomatoes
1 medium can baked beans
salt and pepper
1 level teaspoon flour
1 pound potatoes
4 ounces grated cheese
few drops Tabasco sauce or ½ teaspoon paprika

Mince meat, stir in onions, tomatoes, baked beans, flour, salt and pepper, and place in an ovenproof dish. Peel and thinly slice potatoes and arrange on top. Bake in 350 degree oven for thirty minutes. Sprinkle with cheese and bake for a further fifteen minutes. If not brown, pop under broiler before serving. Four servings.

Schoolboy Omelette

2 pounds potatoes, boiled and
  mashed
For the filling, use one
  of the following:
baked beans
creamed sweet corn

sliced sausages
cooked mushrooms
bacon that has been
  diced and fried crisp
grated cheese
tuna fish in cream sauce

Grease a frying pan well with butter or, better still, bacon fat. Place in potatoes and spread evenly. Cook very slowly until when you lift the side, the underneath looks crisp and brown. Pour filling over and slide on to a plate, folding it in half. Four servings.

Batter Potatoes

2 pounds potatoes
4 level tablespoons plain
  flour
4 tablespoons cold water

pinch of salt
tomato ketchup or grated
  cheese

Parboil potatoes. Peel and cut into thick slices, dusting with salt and pepper. Make a coating batter by mixing flour, salt and water together. Dip each potato slice into the batter and fry quickly in deep fat. Serve with tomato ketchup or grated sharp cheese. Six servings.

Potato Sandwiches

This is a useful way of occupying children on a cold winter's afternoon. Most of it they can make themselves, even doing the frying under supervision.

1 pound mashed potatoes
4 eggs, separated
3 tablespoons milk
teaspoon of salt and
  pepper

tomato sauce
slices of luncheon meat or
  corned beef
flour for dipping

Mix potatoes, 2 eggs, milk and seasonings. Turn half the potatoes on to a wooden board and shape into a rectangle. Spread with tomato sauce and lay on strips of the meat. Cover with the rest of the mashed potatoes, flattening it out with a spatula. Press firm. Cut into sandwiches. Dip first in a saucer of flour, then in the beaten eggs and, finally, in flour again. Fry on both sides in a pan of shallow fat. Four servings.

Peanut Potato Croquettes

2 cups hot riced potatoes	¼ cup soft breadcrumbs
3 tablespoons light cream	¼ cup heavy cream
½ teaspoon salt	¼ teaspoon salt
⅛ teaspoon pepper	⅓ cup chopped peanuts
few grains of cayenne	egg beaten with a little water
few drops of onion juice	dry breadcrumbs
1 egg yolk	or crushed cornflakes

Mix the seven ingredients in the left-hand column together thoroughly. Cook breadcrumbs with cream to make a thick paste and cool. Add peanuts and salt. Make a ball of potato and with your finger make a hole. Fill with nut mixture. Close hole and roll croquettes into an egg-shape. Dip in egg mixture and roll in dry breadcrumbs or crushed cornflakes, being careful that they do not break open. Place in deep fry basket and cook for just under a minute or until golden brown and warmed through. Drain on kitchen towels. Eight servings.

Potato Doughnuts

This recipe is so simple that children can easily make it themselves. Again, I think it is lighter than doughnuts made entirely from flour. Mothers, of course, should supervise the cooking.

½ cup flour	1 egg, beaten
1 rounded teaspoon baking powder	4 tablespoons butter
4 tablespoons sieved, cooked potatoes	

Sift flour and baking powder. Rub in the butter with fingertips. Add potato until it becomes a stiff dough. Lastly, mix in the beaten egg and a little milk if necessary. Roll out until half an inch thick and cut out circles with a wine glass. In the center of each circle cut out a hole with a round cookie cutter. Heat fat until it has blue smoke rising from it. Carefully slide in the doughnuts. Cook for five to seven minutes. Drain on soft paper and dredge with confectioner's sugar. If you prefer ball-shaped doughnuts, roll into a circle, slip a teaspoon of raspberry jam into the center and pinch together the edges to make an air-tight ball. Cook in boiling fat for ten to twelve minutes until golden brown.

Pastry, Flans and Pies

Pastry made with potatoes is delicious, and you can make both puff and short. Not only is it light but the potatoes bind it together so that even though very short, it is easy to handle. I like to use it for all my quiche recipes.

Short Pastry

½ cup self-rising flour
¼ cup finely mashed potatoes
¼ teaspoon salt

6 tablespoons butter or cooking fat (butter is really worth it for special occasions)

Rub all together as in normal pastry making. Bind with just a drop of cold water and leave to stand for an hour or so if possible. This can be used to top meat pies or fruit tarts and is especially good because of its lightness for open hors d'oeuvre tarts.

Puff Pastry

½ cup plus 2 tablespoons self-rising flour
6 tablespoons mashed potatoes

¼ tablespoon salt
3 tablespoons water
½ cup butter

Mix dry ingredients with water to make a firm dough. Leave to firm up for ten minutes in a cool place. Roll into strip and dot butter over two-thirds. Fold into three and roll out. Place in refrigerator for thirty minutes. Take out, turn and roll three more times, placing in refrigerator each time for thirty minutes, and finally leave two or three hours before use. It is even better made the day before and kept in refrigerator overnight.

Quiche Lorraine

potato pastry, according to directions at top of page
2 tablespoons butter
1 small onion peeled and chopped finely
4 ounces streaky bacon cut small

2 eggs
½ cup milk
½ cup heavy cream
salt and pepper
4 tablespoons grated cheese (gruyère is best but cheddar or parmesan will both do)

Line flan ring with pastry and refrigerate while you prepare the filling. Melt butter and sauté onion and bacon slowly until the onion is golden and soft. Beat eggs, milk, cream and salt and pepper to taste. Stir in bacon and onion and pour into flan case. Place in hot oven for five minutes and reduce heat to medium. Cook for about forty minutes. The eggs should be set and golden brown and the pastry light and buttery. Serve sprinkled with chopped chives. Four servings.

Leek Flan

Prepare the same way as for Quiche Lorraine, only substituting two finely cut leeks for the onion and bacon.

Spinach Flan

Put through blender or blend by hand 1 package (sixteen ounces) of spinach with three eggs and a half cup heavy cream. Add salt and pepper to taste. Pour into pastry in flan ring and cook until set, about forty minutes. Parmesan cheese can be sprinkled on top if desired or finely chopped streaky bacon that has been fried until it is crisp, but these are just added refinements. Four servings.

Egg and Asparagus Quiche

Serve as a first course for a luncheon party or buffet supper. It is especially good as an antidote to stodgy winter food.

short pastry, according to directions on page 108
2 eggs
1 large potato, peeled and finely grated

½ cup light cream
salt and pepper
1 package frozen asparagus

Line flan pan with pastry. Beat eggs, grated potato, cream, salt and pepper. Pour into flan and top with asparagus arranged like the spokes of a wheel. Bake for twelve minutes at 450 degrees and reduce to 300 degrees for thirty-five minutes more. Four servings.

Beef, Green Pepper and Mushroom Pie

1 pound stewing steak
½ cup sliced onions
¼ pound sliced mushrooms
1 cup beef stock
1 glass red wine or dark ale

½ cup green peppers, chopped
salt and pepper
1 pound new scraped potatoes
potato puff pastry, from directions on page 108

Cut steak into small chunks and fry in hot fat to seal. Remove, and fry the onions until golden brown. Add mushrooms. Return steak to pan. Pour over all the boiling stock, wine or beer, and add the chopped green pepper, pepper and salt. Cook for three quarters of an hour. Add new potatoes and cook a further ten minutes. Set aside to cool. Place in pie dish, cover with pastry and bake at 450 degrees for thirty minutes. Four servings.

Chicken, Mushroom and Hard-Boiled Egg Pie

4 chicken joints, cooked
4 hard-boiled eggs
¼ pound button mushrooms
4 tablespoons cornstarch
    or flour
chicken stock to cover
salt and pepper
potato puff pastry, from
    directions on page 108

Remove chicken meat from bone and place in pie dish. Lay eggs on top, halved if preferred. Fill gaps with button mushrooms that have been washed but not peeled. With cornstarch, thicken sufficient chicken stock to cover, season, and pour over. Top with potato pastry and bake at 450 degrees for thirty minutes. Four servings.

Southern Chicken Pie

Follow the recipe above but instead of hard-boiled eggs make tiny meat balls from half a pound of sausage meat plus one cup of diced raw potato.

Tuna Fish Pie

½ cup butter
1 sliced onion
4 tablespoons flour
½ teaspoon salt
⅛ teaspoon pepper
1½ cups boiling water
2 crushed chicken bouillon
    cubes
½ cup milk
1 large can tuna fish
1 cup celery or finely diced
    cooked potato
2 hard-boiled eggs, halved
potato puff pastry, from
    directions on page 108

Cook onion and butter for two minutes, add flour, salt and pepper and stir until smooth. Add water and chicken cubes, stir in milk until sauce thickens. Add tuna fish roughly chopped, celery or potato. Lastly top with halved eggs. Cover with potato short pastry or serve with triangles made from potato puff pastry. Four servings.

Sausage and Apple Pie

1 pound cooking apples, peeled
    and sliced
4 tablespoons sugar
2 medium onions, finely chopped
1 pound pork sausage meat
1 cup canned tomatoes, chopped
potato short pastry, from
    directions on page 108

Place apples at bottom of the pie dish and sprinkle with sugar. Mix onion with sausage and spread over the apple. Cover with the tomatoes, juice included. Top with potato short pastry. Four servings.

Puddings,
Cakes and
Bread

It is, of course, quite irrelevant to think that all potato recipes should be cheap. True, most of them are astonishingly inexpensive, but there are time when you can let go. I choose four recipes that are really worthwhile making. The strange thing is that no one would suspect that the base is ordinary mashed potato. They are absolutely memorable.

Potato Chocolate Gateaux

Queen Elizabeth, the Queen Mother, likes marmalade and ground almonds in her chocolate cake, and I have added these ingredients with success.

8 ounces semi-sweet chocolate
2 eggs
4 tablespoons sugar
½ pound melted butter (no substitute will do)
1 teaspoon instant coffee
2 tablespoons dark marmalade

1 cup mashed potatoes
8 ounces sweet biscuits, crushed (I use digestive biscuits but Graham crackers or plain arrowroot biscuits would do just as well)
¼ cup ground almonds

Line a one-pound tin with buttered paper. Melt chocolate in a bowl over water. Meantime, beat eggs and sugar until they are frothy. Stir in butter gently, then melted chocolate, coffee, marmalade, potatoes and crushed biscuits. You must work quickly here before the mixture becomes thick. Pour into dish and leave in the refrigerator for an hour or so before cutting. Decorate with roasted almonds stood upright like teeth, covering the top of the cake.

Kartoffel-Torte

From Berlin, where the torte rates highly as a dessert, comes this mouth-watering recipe for Kartoffel-Torte. I am grateful to my friends, Ruth and Henry Blunden, for this recipe. Theirs is one of the diminishing dinner tables in London where the food and the conversation are always of the same generous quality.

¾ pound boiled, peeled and diced potatoes
¾ pound sugar
9 eggs, separated

¼ pound sweet almonds, finely grated
2 tablespoons bitter almonds, finely grated

Mix all ingredients, except the egg whites, until you achieve a smooth creamy "dough." In a pre-war Berlin kitchen, the mini-cook took half an hour to do it by hand. An electric mixer today takes about five minutes. Fold in stiffly beaten egg whites, and place in a hot oven for three quarters of an hour.

Potato Madeira Cake

1 pound mashed potatoes	4 tablespoons melted butter
½ cup confectioners' sugar	2 eggs, separated
½ cup candied lemon peel or ginger	1 teaspoon vanilla extract
	3 tablespoons Madeira
	milk, if necessary

Mix sugar and lemon peel with potatoes. Add butter. Beat in yolks. Add vanilla and Madeira. Whip up whites until they are stiff and fold in gently. If mixture is too stiff, add a little milk. Pour into a greased eight-inch pie pan. Sprinkle top with lemon peel or preserved ginger. Bake for forty minutes in a 350 degree oven.

If you pine for your grandmother's seed cake, then omit candied fruits and add to mixture 1 teaspoonful of cumin seed.

I would not believe that you could make chocolate éclairs from potatoes, it being seemingly impossible to obtain something as delicate, light and sophisticated. But they are just as good, if not better, than éclairs made from flour, and you cannot taste the potatoes. The one thing about making éclairs for the first time is that you must not have a faint heart. It all looks wrong, but strangely the whole recipe takes shape if you follow it exactly.

Chocolate Eclairs

4 tablespoons butter	2 eggs, each in a saucer
½ cup cold water	⅔ cup sieved potato
5 tablespoons flour	pinch of salt

Melt butter in a saucepan, add cold water and bring to the boil. Remove from heat and add flour and a pinch of salt. Beat until the mixture is smooth and leaves the sides of the pan. Leave to cool for a minute, then add one egg, beating all the time. Add sieved potato and half the other egg—the rest you use for glazing. The mixture is ready when a lump of it is lifted and leaves a three inch trail. Pipe éclairs through a forcing bag or the corner of a paper bag. Canapé éclairs should be piped with a quarter-inch nozzle and chocolate éclairs with a half-inch rose. Make each éclair four inches long. Brush remainder of egg yolk on top of canapé éclairs. Bake in a 400 degree oven for about 25 minutes until they have risen and are a light buff color. Reduce heat to 350 degrees and leave for fifty minutes in all, or until they feel light and dry. Fill with cream when cold and top with chocolate icing. For a change add a drop of essence of mint to the chocolate. For canapé éclairs, make a rich creamy mixture of either tuna fish, salmon, mushroom, sweet corn or sauce mornay. Fill as with chocolate éclairs and serve immediately. If you leave them too long the éclair tends to become heavy and damp.

Potato Kisses

These are just as frivolous as they sound, and can be made before guests arrive. Like the real thing, they are charming to finish a delicious meal. Add two tablespoons sugar and two drops of vanilla to the eclair pastry above. Drop in small spoonfuls into deep fat which is just smoking hot. Cook until golden and puffed out, turning with a fork. Drain on kitchen paper and dredge with sugar. Serve with a fresh raspberry sauce made by putting fresh or deep frozen raspberries in a blender and whizzing until frothy. I prefer them without sugar as the "kisses" are sweet in themselves.

I am not a pudding eater, but there are several great recipes for which the world would be a poorer place if they were to disappear— junket from Jersey milk with cold cream, a fine apple pie with cloves, Queen's Pudding and the Danish Rodgrod med Flode. Some old-fashioned grocers sell potato flour, which lasts for ages in an air-tight container.

Red Pudding

This is a wonderful recipe for the cottage gardener who can walk around on a summer morning picking a handful of this and that. You can adapt the recipe to suit the occasion. But even town shoppers will find it worthwhile. As it is such a family favorite I have given quantities for eight servings.

1⅔ *pounds red currants*	½ *cup potato flour*
1⅔ *pounds raspberries*	*vanilla*
8 *cups water*	*cut almonds*
sugar to taste	*cream*

Wash the currants and raspberries, add water and boil. When all the juice has boiled out, remove from fire and put through a sieve. Sweeten to taste and bring to the boil again. Remove from the fire and thicken with potato flour, using a quarter of a cup to every four cups of juice. If the potato flour boils, the pudding will be "long," a sure sign of a bad cook in Denmark. Add vanilla and pour into a glass bowl. Sprinkle with sugar so that it will not form a skin. Serve very cold, decorated with blanched almonds and lots of cold cream.

Almond Tart

potato short pastry, from
    directions on page 108
raspberry or strawberry jam
4 tablespoons butter

4 tablespoons sugar
2 eggs, beaten
½ cup potatoes, mashed
¼ cup ground almonds

Line an eight-inch pie pan with the pastry and spread with jam. Cream butter and sugar. Add beaten eggs, potatoes and ground almonds. Turn into pie shell, and with any extra trimmings, make a lattice top. Bake in a 425 degree oven for twenty minutes, then reduce to 350 degrees for another twenty-five minutes until the filling is firm. Sprinkle with confectioners' sugar.

And finally, here are two breads, one elaborate, one simple, but both made with Idaho potatoes, which have qualities ideal for the purpose.

Sesame Potato Twist Loaf

½ cup butter
1½ cups sieved hot cooked Idaho
    potatoes
2 tablespoons sugar
2 teaspoons salt
1 cup milk, scalded

2 packages active dry yeast
⅓ cup warm water
5½ cups sifted all-purpose flour
1 egg white slightly beaten
    with 1 tablespoon water
Sesame seeds

In a large mixing bowl, add butter to potatoes, and stir until melted. Add sugar, salt, and milk, and stir until mixture is smooth and cooled to lukewarm. Soften yeast in water, then stir to disolve; stir into potato mixture. Stir in 3 cups of the flour, beating with a spoon until smooth. Gradually stir in enough of the remaining flour to make a moderately firm dough which does not stick to sides of bowl. Turn out on a lightly floured board and knead until smooth and elastic, about 10 minutes, working in only as much additional flour as necessary to prevent dough from sticking (about 1 cup). Place dough in a buttered bowl, turning to butter all sides. Cover and let rise in a warm place (about 85°) until doubled in bulk, about 50 minutes. Punch dough down thoroughly, divide into four parts; roll each between buttered palms to form a strand about 15 inches long. Spiral-wrap two strands together to form a twist-loaf, tucking ends under. Lift into a buttered loaf pan (9 x 5 inches). Repeat with remaining strands. Cover and let rise in a warm place until almost doubled, about 20 to 30 minutes. Gently brush tops of loaves with egg white mixture. Sprinkle generously with seeds. Bake in a 400 degree oven for 10 minutes. Reduce oven heat to 350 degrees and bake for 35 minutes more or until golden brown. Turn loaves out of pans onto a wire rack to cool. Makes two loaves.

O'Brien Baked Potato Bread

Any easygoing Sunday supper can be built around O'Brien Baked Potato Bread. This hearty old-time bread really does have a distinct baked potato flavor when made with Idaho potatoes. It could make your reputation!

1 package dry yeast
2 cups warm water
2 cups grated Idaho baking potatoes
½ cup chopped green pepper
1 large onion, chopped

3 cloves garlic, crushed
4 cups sifted flour
2 teaspoons salt
pinch of sugar
1 egg, lightly beaten

Soften yeast in warm water. Squeeze potatoes dry in paper towels. Add to yeast mixture with rest of ingredients, blending well. Grease a large, heavy skillet with bacon grease or butter; pour in potato mixture and brush top with beaten egg. Cover with a clean towel and let rise in a warm place until double. Bake in a 400 degree oven until top is nicely browned and firm to the touch. Serve with butter. Eight servings.

The Sweet Potato: Up from Aphrodisiac

When Columbus tasted sweet potatoes on his first trip to Hispaniola in 1492, he described them as "looking like yams" (with which he was already familiar) "and tasting like chestnuts." On his return to Spain he was greeted as a hero at the court of King Ferdinand and Queen Isabella at Barcelona. There, amid a glorious celebration, he was received with all the curiosity surrounding astronauts returning from the moon.

A showman, Columbus waved his hand as each exhibit was shown to the amazed court. There were strange new fruits to be touched, smelled and tasted, a fascinating collection of gold, often in the shape of birds with human heads, which had been pillaged from the Inca graves, plus a collection of animals, ten shivering, totally bewildered Indian natives, and baskets of *Impomoea batatas*, the sweet potato.

The sweet potato had in fact been known some hundreds of years before the discovery of America, and was thought to have reached the Marquesas Island from Peru some time in the thirteenth century. Early travelers brought back accounts of these strange roots tasting like marzipan, all through the fourteenth and fifteenth centuries. In various parts of Spain, it was in limited cultivation as early as the sixteenth century.

Probably the Empress Josephine did more to popularize the sweet potato than anyone else in Europe. As a child, Marie-Josephe-Rose Detascher—it was Napoleon who changed her name to Josephine—had been brought up eating sweet potatoes in the fertile French colony of the Martinique Islands. On the family sugar plantation, sweet potatoes were a normal crop. She brought to the pedantic French court her joy in gardening. Under her knowledgeable patronage, public parks and gardens burst into bloom. She introduced some one hundred and eighty species of plants and her exotic choices reflect her homesickness for the tropical islands she had left behind—hibiscus, camellia, purple magnolia, mimosa, geranium and, of course, the sweet potato.

Enraged court beauties, still smarting under the snub that their Emperor had chosen a Creole as his Empress, looked for some ulterior reason. Gleefully they seized on the sweet potato. Why else had the Empress ordered them to be planted in the gardens at Malmaison and Saint Cloud? Were they the secret weapon with which she had lured Napoleon?

Even the fashionable courtesans of the day fell upon the little sweet potato. They plagued the merchant gardeners to keep them supplied in order to titillate their elderly desiccated patrons. To the list of oysters, honey, cock sparrows and the sweet Tokay wine from Hungary, all accepted aphrodisiacs of the day, was added the recipe for slices of sweet potato that had been first boiled or baked and then peeled and dipped in sugar and orange juice. Satiated with the root, alas, the aged counts and marquis were soon to discover that flatulence is no substitute for passion. But the legend lingered on for many years, fanned by news from Ireland of the population explosion that the potato had caused there.

Long before the ordinary potato had reached England, the sweet potato had been imported from Spain and sold in the streets of London around the Royal Exchange as a sucket. They were roasted on embers, much as chestnuts are today. In his conclusive book *The History and Social Influence of the Potato*, Redcliffe Salaman writes:

> *The sweet potato of Spain was not the only, nor perhaps the chief aphrodisiac known as this period, but it was rarely omitted from a dish intended to "incite Venus." It is by no means clear why nor where the sweet potato acquired this character. Its shape, which is often of a somewhat elongated ovoid character, might possibly suggest the likeness of a phallus, seeing that such fantasies are never difficult to conjure up, if the desire so to do is present, but it is doubtful if that is the real basis of the myth. If the shape of the vegetable were the determining factor, then the carrot should have earned a like reputation centuries earlier, but it has escaped that distinction.*

Like most aphrodisiacs the sweet potato was an expensive luxury. In the seventeenth century the sweet potato was sold at something around three shillings a pound, which by today's money is nearer $4. Thomas Moffett, one of the early keep-fit addicts, wrote a book at the end of the sixteenth century called *Health* in which he declared:

> *They nourosh mightily . . . engendering much flesh, blood and seed, but withal encreasing wind and list.*

It was also the sweet potato that inspired Shakespeare, in *The Merry Wives of Windsor*, to make his Falstaff say:

> *My doe with the black scut! Let the sky rain potatoes; let it thunder to the tune of "Green Sleeves," hail kissing-comfits and snow eringoes; let there come a tempest of provocation, I will shelter me here.*

And again it is surely a concupiscent reference when in *Troilus and Cressida*, Thersites exclaims:

> *How the devil luxury, with his fat rump and potato-finger, tickled these together! Fry lechery, fry!*

As sweet potatoes contain more sugar and fat than the normal potato, they are more often used as a pudding. I place them in the same culinary category as pumpkin pie. If you have tasted a poor one you have most certainly been put off for life, but a superbly made pumpkin pie can be a tremendous experience.

The moral is, do not stint on the ingredients for any of the following sweet potato recipes. When it says butter use butter and when it says brandy then only rum or whisky can be substituted.

When shopping for sweet potatoes, select those with smooth skins. If there are little rootlets attached, the sweet potato will be fibrous and unpalatable. Sweet potatoes are lighter in color and have a more mealy flesh than yams, which display deep orange flesh and are soft and moist when cooked. Yams are best steamed, baked, sautéed, deep fried and mashed. Sweet potatoes are best for roasting, boiling and candying, and for pies, cakes and puddings.

In France the Malaga pink sweet potatoes are grown and made into delicate jam. Small ones are preserved in syrup and served in place of marrons glacé.

Here are three recipes for Candied Sweet Potatoes: one from my native New Zealand, where it is called Kumara by the Maoris, one from Jamaica, which has specialized in sweet potato recipes for several hundred years, and one from America.

Candied Sweet Potatoes from New Zealand

1 pound sweet potatoes, peeled	½ cup brown sugar
¼ pound apricots (use only dried apricots as canned ones are too sickly), cooked and drained, saving the liquid	4 tablespoons melted butter
	¼ cup liquid from the apricots
	1 teaspoon grated rind of orange

Cut potatoes into thick slices and arrange in a casserole. Cover with a layer of apricots. Sprinkle with part of the brown sugar. Repeat layers, finishing with one of sweet potatoes. Mix butter, apricot liquid and orange rind and pour over potatoes. Bake uncovered for forty-five minutes, basting twice, in a 350 degree oven. Serve with chilled whipped cream. Four servings.

Candied Sweet Potatoes from Jamaica

1½ pounds sweet potatoes	⅔ cup imported golden syrup or light corn syrup
⅔ cup fresh lime or, at a pinch, lemon juice	1⅓ cups dark brown sugar
	1⅓ cups hot water

Peel potatoes and cut in half lengthwise, leaving in boat shape—small potatoes are the best. Blanch in boiling water for ten minutes. Remove from water and place in a baking pan. Mix syrup with lime juice, sugar and hot water, and pour over potatoes. Place in 350 degree oven and bake, basting until golden brown and candied. Four to six servings.

Candied Sweet Potatoes from America

4 medium-sized sweet potatoes   ⅔ cup brown sugar
4 tablespoons butter   ⅛ cup water

Boil potatoes, pare and cut in halves lengthwise. If using large potatoes cut through the center as well. Heat butter and brown sugar in a heavy frying pan and add potatoes, keeping the pan moving so that they tumble and brown on both sides. Add water and reduce heat and cook until tender (about thirty-five minutes). Just before serving pour half a cup of warmed brandy over and light with a match so that it flames. Four servings.

Sherried Sweet Potatoes

4 medium-sized sweet potatoes   cream to moisten
3 tablespoons butter   sherry to taste
salt

Bake potatoes in the oven until they feel soft, for about one hour. Scoop out insides and add salt, butter, cream and sherry to taste, Refill skins and bake in 400 degree oven for five minutes. I cheat and top up on the sherry just before serving, and on party occasions sprinkle with roasted almonds. Four servings.

Sweet Potatoes with Orange and Lemon

2 pounds sweet potatoes   ⅔ cup brown sugar
1 orange   ⅓ cup water
1 lemon   cinnamon (optional)
4 tablespoons butter

Dice potatoes in half-inch squares. Slice orange and lemon paper-thin. Butter an oven-proof dish and arrange potatoes and fruits in layers. Sprinkle with sugar and dot with the butter. Add water. Cover with foil and bake in a 350 degree oven for one hour until tender. For a more spicy taste sprinkle cinnamon on the top. Six servings.

Glazed Sweet Potatoes

2 pounds sweet potatoes
4 tablespoons butter

2 tablespoons imported golden
syrup or light corn syrup

Boil or steam sweet potatoes and peel. Cut into pieces about two inches long. Melt butter in a saucepan and add potatoes and syrup, turning occasionally until the glaze has covered all sides. Serve piping hot. Eight servings.

Some flavors and textures in cooking are simply made for each other. I like the combination of sweet potato and orange, dating as far back as Elizabethan times. I invariably add grated orange rind to all my sweet potato vegetables recipes, but if you prefer a more spicy taste for serving with roast duck, for instance, add a few grains of nutmeg, allspice and cinnamon.

Mashed Sweet Potatoes

4 medium sweet potatoes
6 tablespoons butter
½ teaspoon salt

orange juice to moisten
1 tablespoon grated orange peel

Boil potatoes, peel, and rice or mash when hot. Add other ingredients and beat until light.

Mashed sweet potatoes are delicious served with baked ham, and Americans eat them with the Thanksgiving turkey, as an alternative to the traditional candied sweet potatoes; though in both cases I find the sweet turkey meat and sweet potatoes together are too much of a good thing. Even sweeter, but a sumptuous variation found at some Thanksgiving feasts, is this delicacy:

Thanksgiving Pineapple Potatoes

Add to 1 pound mashed sweet potatoes two well-beaten eggs and half a cup of drained, crushed pineapple. With a tablespoon make into small patties and fry until golden brown on each side.

Sweet Potato Puffs

Take the mashed potato mixture, omitting the orange rind, and with floured hands shape into small balls as big as plums. Roll in cornflakes, crisp streaky bacon crumbs or chopped almonds. Bake in 350 degree oven until brown.

Sweet Potato Marshmallow Puffs

Americans delight in using marshmallows in the most unexpected ways. Frankly I find this recipe too sweet, although served as a luncheon dish, with crispy bacon and a cool crisp green salad, it is quite amusing. The marshmallows give a gooey center.

Using the same recipe as for mashed potatoes, omit the orange rind and mold the sweet potato around half a marshmallow. Roll in cornflakes, chopped almonds or biscuit crumbs and bake in a 350 degree oven.

Creole Sweet Potatoes

The Empress Josephine was most likely to serve her sweet potatoes as a separate course, and with honey, which is typical of Creole cooking.

Boil or steam four medium-sized potatoes and dry off in the oven. Just before serving, split potatoes open and dab with butter and a spoonful of honey.

Fried Sweet Potatoes

This is another Creole specialty, and simply delicious with sausages, bacon or ham. Peel and slice one pound of boiled sweet potatoes. Fry in hot fat until golden brown and serve with a sprinkling of vanilla sugar.

Sweet Potatoes l'Imperiale

Henri Charpentier was a small French pageboy in the Hotel Cap Martin when the Riviera was still a beautiful and elegant playground for the very rich. When he grew up and became a famous chef he took himself to America, where his round, rosy, smiling face and delicacy of touch made him a friend of such millionaires as Commodore William K. Vanderbilt, "Diamond" Jim Brady and Theodore Roosevelt. In his own restaurant he titillated their jaded palates and gained immortality! Henri's recipe for Sweet Potatoes l'Imperiale deserves a place of honor in every kitchen. It is especially good with game or venison.

Butter an oven-proof dish and put in sliced raw sweet potatoes, tart cooking apples and bananas. Henri suggests equal quantities, but this you can vary according to taste. Mix all together and season with salt and pepper and paprika. Dot with small pieces of butter, cover with foil and bake in a 300 degree oven for one hour. Take out of the oven and spread with apricot purée.

Once you have accepted the sweet potato as a pudding there are no end of variations. It is a much more versatile food than chestnuts for instance, and look what the French have done with *them!*

Sweet Potato Cake

1 pound sweet potatoes, boiled and peeled
2 eggs
½ cup confectioners' sugar
4 tablespoons melted butter

milk (if necessary)
½ cup candied peel or pineapple cut up very finely or ground almonds
sugar for dusting

Rice potatoes into a basin and mix in sugar, peel or almonds, and butter. Separate eggs and mix in beaten yolks. Whisk whites until stiff, fold into the mixture, adding a little milk if it appears too dry. Pour into a greased eight-inch sandwich tin. Bake in a 350 degree oven until golden brown. Sprinkle with sugar, and serve hot or cold. If served hot, any chocolate, butterscotch or fruit sauce is a good accompaniment. Four servings.

Jamaican cooks have developed a high skill in cooking yams, bananas and the sweet potato. In the outskirt villages, the Jamaican still prefers to boil or bake his sweet potato, peel it and eat it like an apple. But in the more sophisticated hotels bulging with demanding, spoiled tourists the sweet potato is unrecognizable. Pone is a North American Indian word for a light bread, and is usually made from corn.

Jamaica Sweet Potato Pone

1 coconut grated to yield 2½ cups coconut milk
3 cups hot water
1½ pounds uncooked sweet potato
⅔ cup brown sugar

large pinch nutmeg
1 teaspoon cinnamon
⅔ cup raisins
1 tablespoon currants
2 teaspoons vanilla
1 tablespoon butter
whipped cream

Express the milk from the grated coconut by adding half the hot water at a time, allow to soak for ten minutes, and then squeeze until two and a half cups have been obtained. Grate the sweet potato on a fine grater, and combine with milk, sugar, spices, raisins and currants. Add vanilla and butter. Pour mixture into a buttered oven-proof dish and bake in a 350 degree oven for one hour. Serve lukewarm or cold, with whipped cream. Four servings.

Here is a simplified and less rich recipe for the same delicious bread, and ideal for morning coffee parties.

Coffee Party Pone

½ grated coconut
1 pound sweet potato
1 tablespoon cocoa
1 beaten egg

2 tablespoons butter
dash of black pepper
½ cup water
2 tablespoons brown sugar

If you cannot get a fresh coconut, use ½ cup of canned shredded coconut instead, soaking it for half an hour in half a cup of milk. Boil, peel and rice or mash sweet potato. Add remaining ingredients (using the water only if you are mixing in the fresh coconut) and place in a "pudding pan," as the Jamaicans call an oven-proof dish. Bake in a 350 degree oven until firm, for about one hour. Four servings.

Sweet Potato Charlotte

1½ pounds sweet potatoes
1 tablespoon vanilla sugar
2 tablespoons flour
milk to soften
4 eggs

⅔ cup seedless raisins soaked in rum
grated rind of 1 orange
heavy cream or custard

Boil potatoes in unsalted water until soft. Peel and mash to a fine paste, adding sugar and flour gradually. Soften with a little milk. Break in eggs one by one, keeping back two whites which should be whipped stiffly and folded into the mixture at the last moment. Fold in raisins and orange rind lightly. Pour into buttered charlotte mold and cook in a bain marie (pan of hot water) until set. It takes about half an hour. Serve with custard or cream. Eight servings.

Sweet potatoes are much more versatile than most cooks give them credit for. They can be served in place of the ordinary potato, as piquant and delicious vegetables with the meat or game course and as puddings and cakes.

In the vegetable category, I like the Maoris' way of cooking sweet potatoes the best. Even if you do not especially like them, half the fun is in preparing them. First you prepare a nest of stones on the ground, and then light a fire. When the embers have died down the kumara or sweet potato is then wrapped in palm leaves like a parcel and placed on the stones, covered with a wet sack and left to steam for several hours.

If you have little to do and are so disposed, serve them with freshly roasted suckling pig. That is real food for you.

In Rotorua, the thermal region of New Zealand, nature has simplified cooking. With your parcel under one arm, you merely find a steaming pool and leave it there to cook itself.

The sweetness and delicate flavor of the sweet potato go well with all game, veal and pork dishes.

Grandmama Bernell's Sweet Potato Pie

Grandmama Evelyn Bernell was seventy-eight years old when I met her, and lives in Charleston, South Carolina. From her mother, a plantation cook on Edisto Island, she learned to make Sweet Potato Pie. When she was a jazz singer in Florida during the Prohibition Days, it was her pie as much as her singing that attracted the customers. Like all great cooks, Grandmama Bernell cooks on instinct. To watch her in her kitchen is an enriching experience as she goes about popping in a pinch of this, a drop of that. No pie is quite the same—as if each one was part of Grandmama Bernell's soul. Here is her pie recipe captured on one of her great big happy days.

1½ cups mashed sweet potatoes	1 cup milk (or orange juice)
1 egg, beaten	rum, if you have it
2 tablespoons butter	sugar to taste
¼ teaspoon salt	rich, short pastry crust, such as the recipe on page 108

Line an eight-inch flan ring with the pastry, saving enough to cut into strips and place like lattice over the top of the pie. Mix all the other ingredients together, turn into the pastry shell and decorate with the remainder of the pastry. Bake in a 350 degree oven for twenty-five to thirty minutes.

My friend, American writer Dawn Langley Simmons, has sent me the next four recipes from her favorite Southern cookbook.

Spicy Sweet Potato Cake

¼ pound butter	1 teaspoon each cloves, allspice, nutmeg, cinnamon and vanilla
1 pound sugar	
4 eggs	
4 cups sifted flour	1½—2 cups mashed sweet potatoes
2 heaped teaspoons cocoa	
1 teaspoon bicarbonate of soda	1 cup buttermilk
1 teaspoon baking powder	½ pound chopped nuts
1 teaspoon salt	¾ cup raisins

Cream butter and sugar well, add eggs, one at a time, beating well. Add part of flour to nuts and raisins. Add rest of dry ingredients to flour. Add alternately with milk and sweet potatoes to creamed mixture, beating well. Lastly, add nuts and raisins. Bake in a well-greased flat tin in a 300 degree oven for about one hour and twenty minutes.

Sweet Potato Coconut Pudding

½ cup white sugar
⅔ cup brown sugar
1 cup milk
2 cups grated raw sweet potatoes
2 eggs

½ cup melted butter
¼ cup raisins
½ pound pecan nuts or walnuts
½ cup coconut

Combine all ingredients, mixing well. Bake in a 350 degree oven for one hour.

South Carolina Sweet Potato Pie

1⅛ cups dark brown sugar
½ teaspoon salt
1½ teaspoons ginger
1½ teaspoons cinnamon
1½ cups milk

2 cups mashed sweet potatoes
2 eggs, beaten
2 tablespoons melted butter
9 inch deep-dish pie shell

Use your favorite pie crust recipe. Line a deep pie dish with the pastry. Mix sugar, salt and spices. Combine all ingredients, mixing thoroughly. Pour into pastry shell. Bake in a 425 degree oven for ten minutes, reduce heat to 350 degrees and bake for another hour.

Sweet Potato Surprise

1 pound parboiled sweet potatoes
1⅛ cups brown sugar
1½ teaspoons cornstarch
¼ teaspoon salt
⅛ teaspoon cinnamon

1 teaspoon grated orange peel
1 pound can apricot halves (save juice)
2 tablespoons butter
½ cup pecan nuts or walnuts

Peel potatoes, dice in one-inch squares and place in baking dish. Put brown sugar, cornstarch, salt, cinnamon and orange peel in a saucepan. Stir in one cup of apricot juice (or all the juice you have—I don't usually have quite a cup). Cook to boiling. Add apricots, butter and nuts. Pour over potatoes. Bake in a 350 degree oven for thirty-five minutes. Four servings.

Yam and Ham Supper Dish

2 tablespoons oil
1 cup diced cooked ham
2 cloves garlic, minced
¼ cup chopped celery leaves
4 cups cubed, pared yams
(about 3 medium yams)
2 tomatoes, peeled, seeded, chopped

¾ teaspoon dried leaf thyme
6 cups beef bouillon made from cubes or stock concentrate (or 3 cans condensed beef bouillon diluted with water to make 6 cups)
salt and pepper to taste
grated parmesan cheese

Heat oil in a large saucepan, add ham, garlic and celery leaves, and cook until ham is lightly browned, about 3 minutes. Add yams, tomatoes, thyme and bouillon; bring to a boil, reduce heat and simmer covered 15 minutes or until yams are tender. Season with salt and pepper. Serve with parmesan cheese. Six main-dish servings.

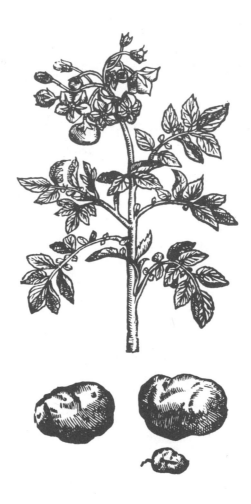

A Final Fillip

A FINAL FILLIP: KISSES AND WINE

Potato Fondant Kisses

These are super-nutritious, as candies go, because of the combined virtues of the powdered milk and the potato.

1 *potato, medium*
1 *teaspoon vanilla extract*
2 *tablespoons butter*
1 *cup confectioners' sugar*

½ *cup powdered milk*
  (not instant)
melted chocolate for dipping

Peel and steam the potato. Mash it well, and while it is still fairly hot, add the vanilla and butter, stirring well. Sift together the sugar and powdered milk, add these to the potato mixture, stir well, and chill in the refrigerator. After it is chilled, knead enough additional powdered milk into it to allow you to shape small pieces into kisses, or other shapes. Dip each into chocolate melted in a double boiler and cooled to about 83 degrees.

Potato Wine (Poor Man's Rhine Wine)

8 *cups sugar*
4 *quarts water*
3 *pounds of old potatoes (Idahos are wonderful for this wine)*
2 *cups muscat raisins, finely chopped*

6 *thin-skinned oranges, cut into quarter-inch slices*
3 *lemons cut into quarter-inch slices*
1 *package dry granulated yeast*

Put water and sugar into a very large, heavily enameled or porcelainized kettle. Bring to boil over low flame, stirring until sugar is dissolved to prevent scorching. Scrub potatoes well, removing any eyes that may hold dirt. Slice about ¼″ thick. When sugar and water mixture has reached boiling point remove from stove and stir in potatoes, chopped raisins, and sliced lemons and oranges. Cool to lukewarm, and sprinkle yeast over surface. Cover and put in warm place for two weeks, stirring twice each week during this fermentation.

Strain through jelly bag and return liquid to washed, scalded and cooled fermenting vessel to settle for three days. Then siphon into clean, sterilized bottles, stopper with cotton (sterile) plugs until all fermentation has ceased, and seal tightly.

Keep for *at least* six months before using. This wine, when properly aged, is difficult—if not impossible—to tell from a true Rhine wine.

Appendices

Potato Consumption by Country

When the last international survey of potato consumption was taken in 1959, by the Potato Marketing Board, this is how the rating stood. (There are, however, no figures for the U.S.S.R., which is known to be one of the heaviest potato consumers in the world.) The list gives the consumption per head per year, and represents unpeeled potatoes; the following figures have to be reduced by one quarter to find the average weight of potatoes peeled and prepared for cooking.

	kilograms	*pounds*
Poland	250	550
East Germany	220	484
Hungary, Ireland	145	320
Belgium	143	314
Peru	142	312
Denmark	128	281
Spain	124	273
Finland	101	222
France	100	220
Portugal	98	215
Chile	92	202
Ecuador, Netherlands	90	198
United Kingdom, Austria	88	193
Yugoslavia	73	160
Argentina	70	154
China	68	149
Canada	63	138
New Zealand	55	121
Italy	52	114
United States	46	102
Greece	40	88
Cyprus	36	79

Note: By way of comparison, in 1975 the consumption per head in the United States was 118 pounds.

Recommended Daily Intake

Sources of Supply

	Men	Women	Boys	Girls

Percentage contribution to the nutrient content of average household diet

---

ENERGY VALUE OR CALORIES (derived from carbohydrate, fat and protein content)

kcals	kcals	kcals	kcals
3,000	2,200	2,800	2,300

Calories maintain the processes of living: heartbeat, blood circulation, breathing and body temperature. They are used for everyday activities, playing and working.

Potatoes	5%
Milk, cream and cheese	13%
Meat, eggs and fish	19%
Butter, margarine and fat	15%
Bread and flour, cakes, etc.	30%
Other sources	18%

PROTEIN

75g	55g	70g	58g

In addition to contributing to the calorie intake, proteins are needed for growth and repair.

Potatoes	4%
Milk, cream and cheese	23%
Meat, eggs and fish	37%
Bread and flour, cakes, etc.	28%
Other sources	8%

MINERALS

Calcium   500mg 500mg 700mg 700mg

Builds strong bones and hard teeth. Helps clotting of blood. Helps nerves and muscles to work. Helps regulate the use of other minerals in body.

Potatoes	1%
Milk, cream and cheese	61%
Meat, eggs and fish	6%
Bread and flour, cakes, etc.	24%
Other sources	8%

Iron   10mg 12mg 14mg 14mg

Needed by all cells and to form hemoglobin in red corpuscles.

Potatoes	8%
Other vegetables	10%
Meat, eggs and fish	38%
Bread and flour, cakes, etc.	32%
Other sources	12%

Recommended Daily Intake

Sources of Supply

	Men	Women	Boys	Girls

Percentage contribution to the nutrient content of average household diet

---

VITAMIN B GROUP

Thiamine   1.2mg   0.9mg   1.1mg   0.9mg

Improves appetite and digestion. Helps cells to use carbohydrates for energy, keeps heart and nerves healthy.

Potatoes	12%
Milk and cream	15%
Meat, eggs and fish	23%
Bread and flour, cakes, etc.	38%
Other sources	12%

Riboflavin   1.7mg   1.3mg   1.4mg   1.4mg

Keeps mucous membranes and skin healthy, prevents sore mouth and tongue, helps to use oxygen.

Potatoes	3%
Milk, cream and cheese	42%
Meat, eggs and fish	30%
Bread and flour, cakes, etc.	12%
Other sources	13%

	mg	mg	mg	mg
Niacin or	equiv-	equiv-	equiv-	equiv-
Nicotinic	alent	alent	alent	alent
Acid	18	15	16	16

Potatoes	10%
Milk, cream and cheese	15%
Meat, eggs and fish	42%
Bread and flour, cakes, etc.	20%
Other sources	13%

Where there is insufficient nicotinic acid in the diet the growth of children is checked, the tongue becomes red and sore, there is diarrhea and other signs of digestive disorders appear.

VITAMIN C

Vitamin C   30mg   30mg   25mg   25mg

Prevents scurvy. Keeps gums, muscles, skin and bones healthy. Increases resistance to infection.

Potatoes	31%
Other vegetables	20%
Fruit	36%
Milk and cream	9%
Meat, fish and eggs	1%
Other sources	3%

NUTRITIVE VALUES OF THE POTATO*

Food, approximate measure, and weight (in grams)		Water	Food energy	Protein	Fat (total lipid)	Fatty acids			Carbohydrate	Calcium	Iron	Vitamin A value	Thiamine	Riboflavin	Niacin	Ascorbic acid
						Saturated (total)	Unsaturated									
							Oleic	Linoleic								
	Grams	Per cent	Calories	Grams	Grams	Grams	Grams	Grams	Grams	Milligrams	Milligrams	International Units	Milligrams	Milligrams	Milligrams	Milligrams
Potatoes, medium, about 3 per pound:																
Baked, peeled after baking —— 1 potato	99	75	90	3	Trace	——	——	——	21	9	.7	Trace	.10	.04	1.7	20
Boiled:																
Peeled after boiling —— 1 potato	136	80	105	3	Trace	——	——	——	23	10	0.8	Trace	0.13	0.05	2.0	22
Peeled before boiling —— 1 potato	122	80	90	3	Trace	——	——	——	21	9	.7	Trace	.11	.04	1.4	20
French-fried, piece 2 by ½ by ½ inch:																
Cooked in deep fat, ready to eat. —— 10 pieces	57	45	155	2	7	2	1	4	20	9	.7	Trace	.06	.04	1.8	8
Frozen, ready to heat for serving. —— 10 pieces	57	64	95	2	4	1	1	2	15	4	.8	Trace	.08	.01	1.2	10
Mashed:																
Milk added —— 1 cup	195	80	145	4	1	——	——	——	30	47	1.0	50	.17	.11	.2	17
Milk and butter added —— 1 cup	195	76	230	4	12	7	4	Trace	28	45	1.0	470	.16	.10	1.6	16
Potato chips, medium, 2-inch-diameter. —— 10 chips	20	3	110	1	7	2	2	4	10	6	.4	Trace	.04	.02	.6	2

* USDA Home and Garden Bulletin No. 72, "Nutritive Value of Foods," 1971

Index to Recipes

Designed by Schneider Design Associates, Inc.
Composed by the Service Composition Company, Baltimore, Maryland
in Century with display lines in Ultra Bodoni and Cooper Black
Color separation by Graphic Technology, Inc., Fort Lauderdale, Florida
Printed by the John D. Lucas Printing Company, Baltimore, Maryland
on 70 lb. Glatfelter Offset Natural White and Mead Offset Enamel Dull Finish